W9-CPW-208

The sequel to the popular "Splendid Low-Carbing for life (volume-1)"

SPLENDID LOW-CARBING for Life (vol-2)

Another Splendid Guide for Low-Carbing

By Jennifer Eloff
National Best-selling Cookbook Author

Splendid Low-Carbing and *More Splendid Low-Carbing*
Splendid Low-Carbing for Life (vol-1 and vol-2)
Splendid Low-Carb Desserts
Splendid Desserts and *More Splendid Desserts*

Canadian Cataloguing in Publication Data
Eloff, Jennifer, 1957
Splendid Low-Carbing for Life (vol-2)
First Printing ~ November 2004
ISBN 0-9763374-0-1 Includes Index.
1. Low-carb diet recipes. 2. Sugarless recipes.
3. Desserts, cooking and baking low-carb recipes.
4. Title 7. Another Splendid Guide for Low-Carbing.

DEDICATION: This cookbook is dedicated with love and grateful, humble thanks to God, to my family and friends. Thank you also to all my fellow low-carbers, who enjoy and buy my cookbooks.

Photography: Ian Eloff and Ross Hutchinson
Front and Back Cover Design: Ian and Jonathan Eloff
Web-site Enhancements: Daniel and Ian Eloff
Printed by: Houghton - Boston

Pictured on front cover: Apple-Peach Lattice Pie and Bumble Berry Tart
Pictured on back cover: Peaches & Cream Scones, Peanut Butter Cups, Pumpkin Cake Roll, Cheddar Biscuits, Corn Bread, Pumpkin Cheesecake, Brownie

Published by **Eureka Publishing**

Copyright © Jennifer Eloff, 2004

All rights reserved. The use of any part of this publication reproduced, transmitted in any form or by any means, electronic, mechanical, recording or otherwise, or stored in a retrieval system, without the prior consent of the publisher, is an infringement of the copyright law. In the case of photocopying or other reprographic copying of the material, a license must be obtained from the Canadian Copyright Licensing Agency (CANCOPY) before proceeding.

CONTENTS

HELPFUL HINTS

1. *Large eggs* are used unless otherwise specified.

2. *Salted butter* is used unless otherwise specified. *Olive oil* used is a light-tasting olive oil – not the green, strong-tasting kind.

3. *Fermented soy sauce* in moderation does not affect thyroid function adversely. Do some research using Google search engine to confirm this.

4. I usually include in each new book 4 or 5 *old recipes* from previous cookbooks, that will be required, for convenience, as well as for those folks who could only afford to buy one of my cookbooks.

5. A couple of recipes in this book use *sugar free chocolate chips.* I used the net carb calculation given by the manufacturer and this article explains why: atkins.com/Archive/2001/12/26-133646.html Where I used maltitol crystals (2 recipes), I counted half the total carbs. Now there are chocolate chips available by Carbsense.com called Minicarb® Chocolate Chips that are sweetened with sucralose only and no sugar alcohols.

6. *Biskmix^{TM}*, page 65 is an exciting new biscuit mix that may be used almost anywhere Bisquick® is used in old favorite recipes. It will not work so well for Cinnamon Rolls (see page 116, Splendid Low-Carbing for that), which should be more dough-like, and I suspect it will be problematic in most yeast applications. It tends to be a truly biscuit-like mix. That said, it still makes great cobbler and scones. It would appear that impossible pies are "possible," however, the resulting crust (if it is meant to form one) will be a little lighter in texture. Have fun with it!

7. To mimic *brown sugar*, I sometimes suggest using a tiny amount of molasses, however this addition in a recipe is usually optional.

8. Da Vinci® Sugar Free "Kahuli Caffe" Syrup has changed to "Kahlua" Syrup. I make use of these low-carb syrups occasionally. Many recipes can be made using the vanilla flavor instead. Typically, I give alternatives.

9. This time I included a *Western Chinese Cooking* section and skipped the Fish and Shellfish section. Atkins Nutritionals has tips and suggestions for choosing Chinese dishes: atkins.com/Archive/2001/12/17-614000.html

MY PANTRY ETC.

I thought this time around I would give low-carb cooks a peek into my pantry, refrigerator and freezer. Among these are ingredients used to make recipes in my cookbooks. I don't have all the foods on hand all of the time; however, I've marked the foods I generally do have in the house most of the time with an asterix. Some of the items are not low-carb, but keep in mind I still have a teenage son at home and some of the items I use sparingly in low-carb recipes as well. I've also indicated where I buy some of these food stuffs, if it is not immediately obvious. In order to make sure I don't run out of ingredients, I keep a magnetic notepad on the refrigerator, on which I jot down items I am running out of. The next time I go grocery shopping, that list goes along with me for replenishing my stock. It's a simple system; a good way of remaining organized.

In the pantry (some items as indicated are kept in the freezer):
Flours, thickeners and ingredients for bake mixes and other mixes:
*Ground almonds {grocery store, health food store and King Arthur Flour website (Baker's Catalogue)} - freezer
*Ground hazelnuts (health food store and King Arthur Flour website) - freezer
*Natural Whey protein powder (Gym Bag, Canada)
*Vanilla and Chocolate Whey protein powder (Costco, Canada)
*Vital wheat gluten (health food store and King Arthur Flour website)
*Spelt, whole wheat pastry flour, oat flour (grocery & health food store)
*All-purpose flour
*Flax meal (grocery and health food store) - freezer
*Guar Gum and Xanthan gum (health food store)
*Arrowroot powder, for Thickening Agent (health food store)
*Cornstarch (for Thickening Agent)
*Thickening Agent (homemade)
*ThickenThin not/Starch® by Expert Foods (health food store)
*Wheat bran
*Oat bran (grocery and health food store)
*Quick-cooking oats
*Dutch processed cocoa powder (health food store)
*Splenda Granular (Costco, Canada)
*Splenda packets (Sam's Club, U.S.)
*Soy flour and soy protein isolate (I don't use these in books after More Splendid Low-Carbing – available in upscale grocery stores and in health food stores)
*Skim and whole milk powder (health food store, grocery store and Wal-Mart)
*Baking powder and baking soda
*Confectioner's Sugar Substitute (homemade)

*Hot chocolate drink mix (homemade)
*Hot mocha drink mix (homemade)
*Vital Ultimate Bake Mix (homemade with spelt flour)
*Vital Oat Ultimate Bake Mix (homemade)
*Low-Carb Bake Mix (homemade)
*Miscellaneous Bake Mixes from my cookbooks

*Nuts, seeds and dried fruit: Almonds (different cuts), macadamia nuts (occasionally), cashews, hazelnuts, walnuts (and crumbs), pecans, sunflower seeds, pumpkin seeds, sesame seeds (grocery store and health food store), California raisins, sultanas, dried apricots and dates.

*Various Herbs and spices :
(Mrs Dash® seasoning blends, oregano, basil, mild chili powder, hot chili powder, turmeric powder, cumin, parsley, paprika, cardamom, allspice, nutmeg, garam masala, crushed red pepper, rosemary, Italian seasoning, ground anise seed, curry powder (homemade), pumpkin pie spice (homemade), chives, dried onions, seasoning salt, onion salt, garlic powder, white pepper, black pepper, salt, thyme, ginger, cinnamon sticks, ground cinnamon, cayenne pepper, dry mustard, steak spice, chives, dill, peppercorns, taco seasoning (homemade), cloves (whole and ground) and ground coriander.

*Various extracts: Vanilla, almond, maple, chocolate, butterscotch, lemon, orange, peppermint, rum, brandy, pineapple and cherry, etc.

Canned goods: *Tomato sauce, tomato tidbits, crushed tomatoes, *tomato paste, tomato juice, *evaporated milk, *green chilies, *olives, *tuna, *salmon, *ham, *crab meat, *pumpkin, *low-carb spaghetti sauce, *Carnation® or Nestle® thick cream (Wal-Mart, Mexican section, or grocery store), beef and chicken broth and *canned fruits (see under fruit) and *vegetables (see under vegetables).

Miscellaneous Pantry Items:
*Hot pepper sauce
*Liquid smoke (grocery store)
*Wasa® Crackers
*Non-hydrogenated wholegrain crackers (grocery store)
*Cocoa butter {King Arthur Flour website (see baking catalogue – good price) and health food store}
*Unsweetened baking chocolate (grocery store)
*Nonstick cooking spray
*Instant chicken and beef stock mix (grocery store)
*Da Vinci® Sugar Free Syrups (United Grocers Cash and Carry, U.S., some coffee shops & perhaps Wal-Mart
*Cream of tartar

*Active dry yeast
*Worcestershire sauce
*Boxed diet instant puddings
*Unflavored gelatin and sugar free jellies
*Kool-aid® (sugar free)
*Unsweetened, desiccated coconut, medium and fine (health food store)
*Different type of teas, instant and regular ground, caffeinated black tea and decaffeinated herbal teas (grocery stores, kitchen stores & coffee shops)
*Decaffeinated coffee – instant and regular ground
*Coconut milk (grocery store)
*Coconut oil (health food store)
*Molasses
*Sugar (for yeast to consume in breads)
*Low-carb pasta
*Grape-Nuts cereal (for adding to some crusts)
*Cooking Sherry
*Maltitol crystals (www.abountifulharvest.net/maltitol.asp)
*Slimsweet (www.trimedica.com)
*Imitation Honey (Wal-Mart)
*Chocolate chips (sugarless) – (candy store and www.carbsense.com)
*White, red wine and apple cider vinegar
Non-hydrogenated shortening (health food store)
*Olive oil (light tasting variety)
*No sugar needed fruit pectin
*Diet soda pop

In the refrigerator:
Dairy: *eggs (large and extra-large), *milk, *cheese (usually Cheddar, Mozzarella, Swiss, Monterey Jack, Parmesan and Feta cheese), *cream cheese (regular and/or light), *butter (salted and unsalted), *healthy butter (homemade), *yogurt (plain), *sour cream, cottage cheese, ricotta cheese, *whipping cream, cream cheese spread and buttermilk.
Miscellaneous:
*Leftover Biskmix™, page 65 (homemade)
*Bread machine yeast
Ginger root
*Low-Carb Barbecue sauce (homemade)
*Low-carb ketchup (grocery and health food store, sometimes homemade)
*Mustard (Dijon and regular)
*Horseradish
*Low-carb tortillas (homemade or Costco)
*Low-carb bread (homemade or Costco)
*Peanut butter (grocery store and health food store)

*Almond butter (grocery store and health food store)
*Low-carb jams (homemade)
*Crushed garlic
*Soy sauce
*Mayonnaise (sometimes homemade)
*Lemon and lime juice
*Sugar free pickles and jalapenos
*Diet soda pop
*Carbonated water
*Salad dressings (homemade and grocery store)
*Wheat germ
*Salsa
*Chutney (homemade and grocery store)
*Bacon and sliced ham
*Roast Chicken (Costco)
*Baked goodies and/or desserts

Vegetables (buy according to recipes I have planned): **Canned:** *mushrooms (sliced, pieces and stems and whole), *asparagus, *water chestnuts (sliced and whole), *baby corn, *green chilies and black beans. **Frozen:** *spinach, *cut green beans, *cauliflower and broccoli. **Fresh:** *Onions, *peppers, jalapenos, *green onions, *lettuce (different kinds), spinach, radishes, zucchini, eggplant, squash, green beans, mushrooms, bean sprouts, *cauliflower, broccoli, *cucumber, *potatoes, *carrots, cabbage, snow peas, and asparagus.

Fruits: **Canned:** *Fruit cocktail, *peaches, *mandarin oranges, *pineapple tidbits and *crushed pineapple. **Frozen:** *Strawberries, *rhubarb, *mixed berries, *blueberries, raspberries and *cranberries **Fresh:** strawberries, *bananas, apples, cantaloupe, honeydew melon, *tomatoes, *California avocadoes, raspberries, blueberries, plums, peaches, apricots, grapes, *oranges, *lemons, kiwis and limes.

In the freezer:
Frozen Miscellaneous Foods: Ice cream (homemade), popsicles (homemade), *frozen homemade baked goodies, *ground nuts, *flax meal, *seeds, *frozen fruit and *frozen vegetables (see appropriate sections for itemized products).
*Beef: Ground beef, different cuts of beef, steak, roasts and sausages.
*Poultry: chicken breasts, legs, thighs, wings, whole chicken or turkey.
*Pork: bacon, pork tenderloin or center cut chops, pork loin pork shoulder roasts, ribs, other pork roasts, ham, pork sausage meat and ground pork..
*Seafood: frozen seafood such as shrimp, scallops, lobster, salmon and cod, however, sometimes I buy fresh salmon and fresh large shrimp or scallops.

HOT MOCHA DRINK MIX
A creamy hot, comfort drink.

1 cup SPLENDA® Granular (250 mL)
1 cup skim milk powder (250 mL)
1 cup Confectioner's Sugar (250 mL)
 Substitute, page 97
$^1/_2$ cup Dutch cocoa (125 mL)
$^1/_4$ cup instant coffee granules (50 mL)

Yield: $3^1/_4$ cups (800 mL)
1 tbsp (15 mL) per serving
16.7 calories
1.2 g protein
0.4 g fat
2.2 g carbs

In medium bowl, combine SPLENDA® Granular, skim milk powder, Confectioner's Sugar Substitute, page 97, Dutch cocoa and instant coffee granules.

Heat water in mug in microwave oven 1 minute and 30 seconds. Using a small whisk, whisk in 1 tbsp (15 mL) or a little more Hot Mocha Drink Mix. Add cream to taste.

Helpful Hints: If desired, add Da Vinci® Sugar Free Syrup, flavor of choice, to further sweeten the drink. I like Da Vinci® Sugar Free Kahlua or Irish Cream Syrup in this drink.

~~Bits & Bites~~
Shelf life of goodies made with SPLENDA® Granular is short, especially in hot weather. Refrigerate baked goods after a day.

CINNAMON TEA

A tea popular in the Middle East. If there are any carbs or calories imparted to the tea, it must be negligible.

3 cups water (750 mL)
1 cinnamon stick
Sweetener to taste

> *Yield:* 2 servings
> 1 serving
> 0 calories
> 0 g protein
> 0 g fat
> *0 g carbs*

In medium saucepan, combine water and cinnamon stick. Bring to a full rolling boil and boil 5 minutes. Remove from heat. Serve immediately and leave cinnamon sticks in leftover tea, if desired.

Helpful Hint: I enjoy this tea with $1\frac{1}{2}$ tsp (7 mL) cream and sweetener.

Fast Facts: A Pakistani study used people with diabetes as subjects. They consumed 1, 3 or 6 g cinnamon daily and had a significant drop in serum glucose, LDL (bad) cholesterol, triglycerides and total cholesterol, but no improvement in HDL (good) cholesterol. Scientists believe cinnamon has a component that may enable it to serve as an insulin substitute in Type 2 Diabetes.

BUMBLE BERRY COOLER

Tasty! Instead of Da Vinci® Syrup, use strawberry sugar free Kool-Aid®, water and sweetener to taste.

1 cup fresh strawberries (250 mL)
$\frac{3}{4}$ cup Da Vinci® Raspberry, (175 mL)
  OR Vanilla Sugar Free Syrup
$\frac{1}{2}$ cup frozen raspberries, (125 mL)
  (unsweetened)
$\frac{1}{4}$ cup frozen blueberries, (50 mL)
  (unsweetened)
$1\frac{2}{3}$ cups carbonated water, (400 mL)
  (chilled)

> *Yield:* 4 servings
> 1 serving
> 24.9 calories
> 0.4 g protein
> 0.3 g fat
> *3.9 g carbs*

In blender, combine strawberries, Da Vinci® Raspberry or Vanilla Sugar Free Syrup, raspberries and blueberries. Blend well. Pour berry mixture into punch bowl or large, glass salad bowl. Stir in carbonated water. Serve over ice.

PINK LADY

A pretty drink for sipping on a hot day.

1 ¼ cups ice cold water, OR (300 mL)
  a little less for a stronger flavor
1 tbsp Da Vinci® Sugar Free (15 mL)
  Watermelon Syrup
1 SPLENDA® packet
1 tsp lemon juice (5 mL)
1 thin slice lemon

Yield: 1 serving	
1 serving	
5.4 calories	
0.0 g protein	
0.0 g fat	
1.4 g carbs	

In tall glass, combine water, Da Vinci® Sugar Free Watermelon Syrup, SPLENDA® and lemon juice. Float slice of lemon on top. Serve immediately.

Variation: **Peach Lady:** Use Da Vinci® Sugar Free Peach Syrup and omit sweetener. If desired, fill glass with carbonated water. (***0.4 g Carbs***)

ICED TEA

Instead of hot tea, this makes a great summertime beverage.

6 tea bags
4 cups boiling water (1 L)

Yield: 5 servings	
1 serving	
1.9 calories	
0.0 g protein	
0.0 g fat	
0.6 g carbs	

In large teapot, place tea bags. Add boiling water and let steep 3 to 5 minutes; remove tea bags. Cool at room temperature at least 2 hours and then refrigerate. Sweeten, as desired, with a carb-free sweetener such as Da Vinci® Sugar Free Syrup. Serve over ice.

Helpful Hint: Do not chill quickly or the tea will turn cloudy.

~~Bits & Bites~~
Remove cakes from the refrigerator 3 hours before serving.

10

MOLTEN CHEESE POTATO SKINS

Jonathan said with delight, "This is a great appetizer. Put it in the book!"

3 lbs potatoes (1.5 kg)
  (about 13 oz (368 g) potato skins)
$1/4$ cup olive oil (50 mL)
1 tsp seasoning salt (5 mL)
$1/4$ tsp paprika (1 mL)
1 green onion, chopped
$1^1/_2$ cups Monterey Jack, OR (375 mL)
  Cheddar cheese

Yield: 6 servings
1 serving
235.9 calories
9.0 g protein
19.0 g fat
6.0 g carbs

Peel potatoes in strips. Set peel aside. Use peeled potatoes to make a scalloped potato casserole or mashed potatoes for family members or friends or a neighbor not on a low-carb diet.

In large bowl, combine olive oil, seasoning salt and paprika. Add potato skins and toss in seasoned oil to coat well. Lay out in single layer on cookie sheets. Bake in 425°F (220°C) oven 15 to 30 minutes, checking every 5 minutes after the 15 minutes have elapsed to remove crisp, golden potato skins.

Once all potato skins are baked to perfection, lay them out once again on cookie sheets and sprinkle with green onion and Monterey Jack or Cheddar cheese. Bake 5 to 10 minutes, or until cheese is molten.

Helpful Hint: These may also be served with a meal in lieu of potatoes.

~~Bits & Bites~~
Most low-carb baked goods freeze well for at least one month. Wrapping loaves in plastic wrap and then foil keeps them well.

CHUNKY GUACAMOLE

This colorful guacamole makes about 3 cups (750 mL) and serves 6 people as an appetizer or 12 people as a dip. The Guacamole Mini-Wraps below are fabulous.

$^2/_3$ cup chopped tomatoes (150 mL)
4.5 oz can green chilies (127 mL)
$^1/_2$ cup finely chopped red onion (125 mL)
$^1/_4$ cup chopped cilantro, (50 mL)
  (optional)
$^1/_4$ tsp crushed garlic, optional (1 mL)
3 ripe, California avocadoes, peeled and
  pitted
2 tsp lime juice (10 mL)
$^1/_2$ tsp (scant) salt (2 mL)
$^1/_4$ tsp white pepper (1 mL)
$^1/_4$ tsp Tabasco sauce (1 mL)
Garnish (optional):
1 tbsp crumbled Feta cheese (15 mL)
Cilantro leaves
Radish slices, chopped

Yield: 6/12 servings
1 serving
168.2/84.1 calories
2.2/1.1 g protein
15.1/7.6 g fat
8.0/4.1 g carbs

In medium bowl, combine tomatoes, green chilies, red onion, chopped cilantro (if using) and garlic (if using).

On dinner plate, roughly mash avocadoes (to remove pit, twist halves in opposite directions) with potato masher or fork. Flavor with lime juice, salt, pepper and Tabasco sauce. Stir avocadoes into tomato mixture until well combined.

Garnish: Place guacamole in an attractive serving dish and sprinkle with Feta cheese, cilantro and radishes, if using.

Variation: Guacamole Mini-Wraps: Place about 1 tsp (5 mL) or a little less in center of each Cottage Cheese Mini-Pancake, page 24. Close on filling and set upright on a serving dish. (*0.7 g Carbs*)

~~Bits & Bites~~
Refrigerate sealed jams or chutneys up to one year or freeze for longer storage.

TORTILLA CRISPS

Good substitute for tortilla corn chips and so easy to make!

10 low-carb tortillas
  (7 to 8-inches (18 to 20 cm)

> *Yield:* 100 tortilla crisps
> 1 tortilla crisp
> 8.0 calories
> 0.5 g protein
> 0.3 g fat
> *0.7 g carbs*

Cut each tortilla in half and each half into 5 wedges. Spread in single layer on cookie sheets and bake in 350°F (180°C) oven 10 to 12 minutes, or until crisp. Check tortilla crisps after 5 minutes of baking time. Serve with your favorite dip, or try Mexican Dip, page 22, *Splendid Low-Carbing.*

Helpful Hints: The low-carb tortillas that I bought came in at 7 grams of net carbohydrate each and that was what I used in the nutritional analysis. However, if you were to use my Oat Tortillas, page 71, the crisps would come in at *0.5 g carbs*. My tortillas are baked in a much shorter time. Check after 5 minutes. Tortilla Crisps may be spread with flavored cream cheese for a snack.

JALAPENO CHEESE SQUARES

These are self-limiting for me as they are very hot and spicy, however, for a milder version, used canned green chilies instead.

2 jalapeno peppers, seeded
 and finely chopped
10 oz grated Cheddar cheese (284 g)
6 eggs, fork beaten

> *Yield:* 36 squares
> 1 square
> 45.8 calories
> 3.1 g protein
> 3.5 g fat
> *0.3 g carbs*

Spread jalapeno peppers in 8-inch (20 cm) square glass baking dish. Cover with Cheddar cheese. Pour eggs over top. Bake in 350°F (180°C) oven 25 to 30 minutes, or until set. Serve cold or at room temperature.

Helpful Hint: Use gloves while handling jalapenos.

SOUPS AND SALADS

HAWAIIAN SHELLFISH SOUP

This recipe practically makes up for the fact that there is no seafood section in this cookbook, due to the inclusion of the Chinese cooking section. I love it! It is very spicy when 1 jalapeno (unseeded) is used, but it is possible to dilute the soup with a mixture of cream and water, thereby further reducing carbs..

$^1/_2$ cup coarsely chopped onion (125 mL)
1 oz fresh ginger (30 g)
$^1/_2$ to 1 jalapeno (seeded)
1 clove garlic (2 mL)
1 tbsp olive oil (15 mL)
$^1/_2$ cup macadamia nuts, optional (125 mL)
14 fl oz Hunts® Tomato Sauce (398 mL)
2 tbsp fresh lemon juice (25 mL)
$1^1/_2$ tbsp paprika (22 mL)
1 cup coconut milk (250 mL)
$^1/_2$ cup water (125 mL)
$^1/_2$ lb frozen, uncooked, peeled shrimp, thawed (227 g)
$^1/_2$ lb frozen and thawed scallops (227 g)

Yield: 6 servings
1 cup (250 mL) per serving
206.0 calories
16.4 g protein
11.6 g fat
9.5 g carbs

In food processor with sharp S-blade, process onion, ginger, jalapeno (stem and seeds removed) and garlic until very finely chopped. In large, nonstick saucepan in olive oil, cook this mixture 8 to 10 minutes, stirring occasionally. Meanwhile in food processor with S-blade, process macadamia nuts until very fine. Add macadamia nuts, tomato sauce, lemon juice and paprika. Cook 2 minutes; add coconut milk and water. Bring soup to boiling point. Add shrimp and scallops. Keep lid on saucepan 5 minutes to allow hot soup to cook shellfish. Be careful not to overcook.

Helpful Hints: If using a larger can of tomato sauce, freeze leftover tomato sauce in a labeled container. Plastic containers will discolor, so use an old one. Freeze remaining coconut milk as well, for making this soup another day. This soup is relatively low in sodium, with the only salt coming from the tomato sauce; however, add salt to taste, if desired. I buy a 1 lb (0.454 kg) combination of frozen shrimp and scallops at my grocery store that is very convenient for this particular recipe.

CONDENSED CREAM OF MUSHROOM SOUP

Good substitute for commercial soup in recipes. This recipe is quick and easy to prepare when required.

1 cup chopped fresh mushrooms (250 mL)
1 tbsp butter (15 mL)
1 cup sour cream (250 mL)
1 tsp dried parsley (5 mL)
1 tsp Mrs Dash® Seasoning (5 mL)
  Blend (Garlic and Herb)
1 tsp SPLENDA® Granular* (5 mL)
$^1/_4$ tsp salt (1 mL)
$^1/_4$ tsp dry mustard powder (1 mL)
$^1/_4$ tsp Worcestershire sauce (1 mL)
$^1/_8$ tsp white pepper (0.5 mL)

Yield: 2 servings
1 serving
243.8 calories
4.7 g protein
22.4 g fat
7.7 g carbs

In skillet, cook mushrooms in butter until soft and liquid has reduced. In small bowl, combine sour cream, parsley, Mrs Dash® Seasoning Blend, SPLENDA® Granular, salt, dry mustard powder, Worcestershire sauce and white pepper. Remove from heat. Add sour cream mixture to mushrooms and stir very well. Use in recipes requiring condensed cream of mushroom soup (double the carbs).

To Serve: Add 1 cup (250 mL) water and bring to boil. Makes 2 servings.

Helpful Hint: *The sweetener is used to reduce any sour taste in the soup.

~~Bits & Bites~~
Use an auxiliary thermometer inside the oven as a backup to make sure oven temperature is correct.

CONDENSED CREAM OF TOMATO SOUP

Excellent substitute for the real thing.

$^3/_4$ cup Hunt's® tomato sauce (175 mL)
$^1/_4$ cup whipping cream (50 mL)
1 tsp SPLENDA® Granular (5 mL)
$^1/_2$ tsp Thickening Agent, page 62 (2 mL)
$^1/_8$ tsp salt (0.5 mL)
$^1/_8$ tsp white pepper (0.5 mL)

Yield: 2 servings
1 cup (250 mL) per serving
126.8 calories
1.9 g protein
10.6 g fat
6.6 g carbs

In medium bowl, combine tomato sauce, whipping cream, SPLENDA® Granular, Thickening Agent, page 62, salt and pepper. Using a wire whisk, whisk until well combined and slightly thickened.

To serve: Add 1 cup (250 mL) water. Heat in the microwave oven until hot. Serve immediately.

Helpful Hints: Use the entire condensed version (double the carbs in above nutritional analysis) in recipes calling for 10.5 fl oz (310 mL) condensed tomato soup. This recipe makes a little less, but not enough to make a big difference. You may need to add extra salt to taste in your recipe requiring tomato soup, as this recipe is low in sodium, comparatively speaking.

This soup will thicken once chilled. Add extra water, if necessary, and heat in microwave oven. Serve with grated Cheddar cheese and ground black pepper, if desired.

~~Bits & Bites~~
Always check baking before first suggested baking time. Pies should be covered with a sheet of foil, if crust is turning brown too quickly.

RED PEPPER SOUP

Light, creamy, pureed soup that is quite mild in flavor.

2 tbsp olive oil (25 mL)
4 red bell peppers, chopped
2 tbsp chopped onion (25 mL)
1 tsp crushed garlic (5 mL)
24 fl oz chicken broth (710 mL)
$^1/_2$ cup whipping cream (125 mL)
$^1/_8$ tsp black pepper (0.5 mL)

Yield: 6 servings
1 serving
156.5 calories
4.0 g protein
12.4 g fat
7.1 g carbs

In large electric frying pan or saucepan, heat oil. Add peppers, onion and garlic. Saute 10 minutes. Pour in chicken broth and reduce heat to low. Simmer 30 minutes. Transfer to a blender and puree until smooth. Pulverize through a strainer and return soup to pan. Stir in cream and black pepper. Heat through. Serve with freshly ground black pepper, if desired.

MARINATED CUCUMBER SALAD

I don't like pickles, because they are so salty and cause me to put on water weight, however, I enjoy this salad, with all the taste and little sodium.

2 medium-sized field cucumbers
$^1/_2$ cup thinly sliced onion (125 mL)
1 cup water (250 mL)
1 cup white vinegar (250 mL)
$^1/_2$ cup SPLENDA® Granular (125 mL)
$^1/_4$ tsp salt (1 mL)
$^1/_4$ tsp black pepper (1 mL)

Yield: 6 servings
1 serving
30.6 calories
1.0 g protein
0.2 g fat
6.7 g carbs

Peel and slice cucumbers thinly, but not quite as thinly as the onion. In medium bowl, combine water, vinegar, SPLENDA® Granular, salt and pepper. Stir in vegetables and leave to marinate at least 3 hours in the refrigerator.

Helpful Hints: There is no knowing how much marinade is actually going to be consumed along with the vegetables, so I assumed in the analysis all of it would be used up, which is not the case, as most of it is left behind when you pick up the vegetables with a slotted spoon. I think it would be safe to assume the carbs indicated above are quite a bit higher than they will be in reality.

SHOPSKA SALAD

A Bulgarian favorite that is just the most beautiful, colorful salad.

4 Roma tomatoes, OR
 medium-sized tomatoes, finely chopped
4 green onions, chopped
Few olives, finely chopped (optional)
1 green pepper, finely chopped
1 red pepper, finely chopped
$^1/_2$ cucumber, finely chopped
$^1/_2$ cup chopped fresh parsley, (125 mL)
 (optional)

Yield: 8 servings
1 serving
75.5 calories
2.1 g protein
5.0 g fat
5.4 g carbs

Dressing:
2 tbsp olive oil (25 mL)
1 tbsp white vinegar (15 mL)
$^1/_2$ tsp salt (2 mL)
$^1/_4$ tsp black pepper (1 mL)
$^1/_3$ cup grated Feta cheese, OR (75 mL)
 more to taste

In large, shallow casserole dish, combine tomatoes, green onions, olives (if using), green pepper, red pepper, cucumber and parsley, if using.

Dressing: In cereal bowl, combine olive oil, vinegar, salt and pepper. Pour over vegetables and toss to combine. Sprinkle with Feta cheese.

Helpful Hints: The green and red peppers may be roasted and the skins removed, if desired. I liked the parsley in the salad, however, my husband and youngest son did not care for it.

~~Bits & Bites~~
Bake mixes, which you can make yourself, are the secret to many of my recipes.
Some are cup-for-cup substitutions for white wheat flour.

PICTURE PERFECT SALAD

This colorful salad is really pretty.

6 cups romaine lettuce (1.5 L)
2 Roma tomatoes, chopped
2 green onions, chopped
1 avocado (use melon baller)
$^1/_2$ cup chopped cucumber, (125 mL)
  (optional)
$^1/_2$ yellow pepper, chopped
2 tbsp crumbled Feta cheese (25 mL)

> *Yield:* 4/6 servings
> 1 serving
> 121.6/81.1 calories
> 3.7/2.5 g protein
> 8.8/6.5 g fat
> *7.5/5.0 g carbs*

Cut romaine lettuce into ribbons (this works best cutting horizontally across at about $^1/_2$ –inch (1 cm) intervals on Romaine hearts). Rinse thoroughly and spin dry in salad spinner. Place in large, glass salad bowl. Arrange tomatoes, green onions, avocado balls, cucumber (if using) and yellow pepper on top. Do not toss. Sprinkle with Feta cheese.

Serve with Creamy French Dressing, page 59 or Honey Mustard Dressing, page 60. Sprinkle with sliced almonds and salted sunflower seeds, if desired.

Helpful Hint: To practically eliminate the risk of E-Coli, thoroughly spray lettuce leaves with white vinegar (5% acetic acid) and rinse with water.

BEET PICKLES

This pretty side dish is my friend, Jenita Davison's, recipe. She says when she takes these pickles to church functions, she seldom returns with any.

$^1/_3$ cup SPLENDA® Granular (75 mL)
$^1/_4$ cup cider vinegar (50 mL)
2 tbsp water (25 mL)
6 whole cloves allspice
$^1/_4$ tsp cinnamon (1 mL)
Pinch of salt
14 oz can sliced beets, drained (398 mL)

> *Yield:* 6 servings
> 1 serving
> 26.1 calories
> 0.6 g protein
> 0.0 g fat
> *5.7 g carbs*

In glass bowl, combine SPLENDA® Granular, cider vinegar, water, cloves allspice, cinnamon and salt. Microwave 2 min. on 70% power. Cool a few minutes and add drained beets. Refrigerate overnight. Pick out allspice cloves.

19

SUMMERTIME STRAWBERRY SALAD

Jelly Layer:
$^1/_2$ cup SPLENDA® Granular (125 mL)
1 envelope sugarless Kool-Aid®
  (strawberry flavor)
1 envelope unflavored gelatin
$^1/_4$ cup cold water (50 mL)
1 cup boiling water (250 mL)
$^3/_4$ cup cold water (175 mL)

Cream Cheese Layer:
8 oz regular cream cheese, softened (250 g)
$^2/_3$ cup SPLENDA® Granular (150 mL)
1 tsp vanilla extract (5 mL)
1 cup half-and-half cream (250 mL)
1 envelope unflavored gelatin
$^1/_2$ cup cold water (125 mL)

Strawberry Jelly Layer:
3 cups fresh strawberries, sliced (750 mL)
$^1/_2$ cup SPLENDA® Granular (125 mL)
1 envelope sugarless Kool-Aid® (strawberry flavor)
1 envelope unflavored gelatin
$^1/_4$ cup cold water (50 mL)
1 cup boiling water (250 mL)
$^3/_4$ cup cold water (175 mL)

> **Yield:** 12 servings
> 1 serving
> 120.9 calories
> 4.2 g protein
> 8.1 g fat
> **7.1 g carbs**

Jelly Layer: In 9 x 13-inch (2 L) glass baking dish, combine SPLENDA® Granular and Kool-Aid®. In cereal bowl, combine gelatin and $^1/_4$ cup (50 mL) cold water. Microwave 40 seconds. Stir boiling water into Kool-Aid® mixture, add dissolved gelatin and $^3/_4$ cup (175 mL) cold water. Chill until set.

Cream Cheese Layer: In food processor or blender, process cream cheese, SPLENDA® Granular and vanilla extract until smooth. While processing, gradually add half-and-half cream. In cereal bowl, combine gelatin and cold water. Microwave on high power 45 seconds. Add to cream cheese mixture. Process briefly. Pour over set jelly layer. Chill about 3 hours or until set.

Strawberry Jelly Layer: Layer strawberries over cream cheese. In medium bowl, combine SPLENDA® Granular and Kool-Aid®. In cereal bowl, combine gelatin and $^1/_4$ cup (50 mL) cold water. Microwave 40 seconds. Pour boiling water over Kool-Aid® mixture, stir in dissolved gelatin and $^3/_4$ cup (175 mL) cold water. Allow to cool. Pour carefully over strawberries. Chill.

BREAKFAST

EGGS WITH A MEXICAN FLAIR

My son, Daniel, loved this breakfast and 2 days later asked for it again.

8 eggs
$^1/_2$ cup Low-Carb Bake (125 mL)
  Mix, page 64
1 tsp baking powder (5 mL)
$^1/_2$ tsp salt (2 mL)
2 cups grated Monterey Jack (500 mL)
  Cheese
1 cup cottage cheese (250 mL)
1 cup grated Cheddar cheese (250 mL)
4.5 oz can chopped green chilies (127 mL)
$^1/_4$ cup medium Salsa (50 mL)

> **Yield:** 15 servings
> 1 serving
> 162.0 calories
> 12.7 g protein
> 11.3 g fat
> *1.7 g carbs*

In food processor or in bowl with electric mixer, process eggs 4 minutes.

In small bowl, combine Low-Carb Bake Mix, page 64, baking powder and salt. Stir into eggs.

In medium bowl, combine grated Monterey Jack cheese, cottage cheese, Cheddar cheese, green chilies and Salsa. Stir egg batter into the cheese mixture and pour into lightly greased 9 x 13-inch (23 x 33 cm) glass baking dish.

Bake in 350°F (180°C) oven 40 minutes, or until set and turning brown. Let cool 5 minutes, before cutting. Serve with extra Salsa, if desired.

~~Bits & Bites~~
My personal favorite bake mix is the Low-Carb Bake Mix, page 64, simply because it produces the lowest carb baking and the baked products taste wonderful as well. I keep it in large, transparent, airtight containers on the counter top in the kitchen.

PUMPKIN WAFFLES

Crispy waffles – great with Low-Carb Pancake Syrup or Strawberry Sauce, page 149, Splendid Low-Carbing, or Peach Syrup, page 61 of this book . Top with Crème Fraiche, page 99.

$2^1/_4$ cups Low-Carb Bake Mix, (550 mL)
   page 64
$^1/_2$ cup SPLENDA® Granular (125 mL)
1 tbsp baking powder (15 mL)
1 tsp cinnamon (5 mL)
$^1/_4$ tsp salt (1 mL)
$^1/_8$ tsp nutmeg (0.5 mL)
2 eggs
$^3/_4$ cup water (175 mL)
$^1/_2$ cup whipping cream (125 mL)
$^1/_2$ cup canned pumpkin (125 mL)
$^1/_4$ cup butter, melted (50 mL)
$^1/_4$ cup olive oil (50 mL)

Yield: 14 waffles
1 waffle per serving
188.7 calories
8.2 g protein
15.9 g fat
3.6 g carbs

Preheat waffle iron according to manufacturer's directions.

In large bowl, combine Low-Carb Bake Mix, page 64, SPLENDA® Granular, baking powder, cinnamon, salt and nutmeg. In medium bowl, whisk eggs. Add water, whipping cream, pumpkin and butter; whisk until well combined. Add to well in center of dry ingredients. Mix well with wooden spoon.

Brush waffle iron interior with some olive oil. Pour $^1/_4$ cupfuls (50 mL) of batter onto center of each section of waffle iron and spread batter with back of spoon to cover. Close lid and cook about 4 to 5 minutes (set timer), or until crispy and brown (do not be tempted to open lid before 4 minutes have transpired). Serve immediately with commercial low-carb pancake syrup of choice or Maple Syrup, page 172, *Splendid Low-Carbing*.

Helpful Hints: To reduce calories, you could use skim or 2% low-carb milk, now available, and use slightly less olive oil to grease the waffle iron.

To reheat waffles later on, pop in the toaster.

~~Bits & Bites~~
My second favorite bake mix is Vital Ultimate Bake Mix, page 66, using either oat flour or whole wheat pastry flour or even spelt flour, depending on the application.

PEACHES AND CREAM SCONES

Scrumptious scones that are great for a change of pace at breakfast time.

4 cups Biskmix™, page 65 (1 L)
 (need to make 2 batches)
1 large egg
$^{1}/_{4}$ cup canned peaches in (50 mL)
 juice, drained
$^{1}/_{4}$ cup SPLENDA® Granular (50 mL)
2 tbsp sour cream (25 mL)

Yield: 12 scones
1 per serving
199.6 calories
10.0 g protein
16.4 g fat
3.5 g carbs

In large bowl, place Biskmix™, page 65. In blender, blend egg, peaches, SPLENDA® Granular and sour cream together. Pour into well in Biskmix™. Stir with wooden spoon to form soft, moist dough. On round pizza pan form an 8-inch (20 cm) circle (it will spread upon baking) using plastic wrap to help press out gently and evenly.

Bake in 425°F (220°C) oven 12 to 15 minutes. Cover with foil after 10 minutes. The scones will be golden brown. Cut scones into wedges. Serve warm. Refrigerate remaining scones (they will become denser and quite good actually). Turn stale scones into Biscotti.

Variations: **Biscotti:** Form a rectangle or large circle of dough on a cookie sheet. Bake as above. Cool half an hour. Slice into biscotti shapes. Lay on ungreased cookie sheet and bake in 325°F (160°C) oven 10 minutes. Flip each biscotti and bake another 10 minutes, or until brown and crisp. Cool on wire racks. If desired, drizzle low-carb white chocolate over biscotti or dip one end in melted white chocolate. If you make 18 biscotti: (***2.4 g Carbs*** each) and if you make 36 biscotti: (***1.2 g Carbs***).

Peach Melba Scones: Slice warm scones in half and spread with low-carb raspberry, strawberry, peach or apricot jam. Top with a dollop Crème Fraiche, page 99, replace top half and enjoy with a cup of hot tea or any hot beverage.

~~Bits & Bites~~
ThickenThin not/Starch by Expert Foods may be used instead of my Thickening Agent, page 62 in recipes.

ULTRA LOW-CARB CREPES

Ultra tasty too! Lovely with Crème Fraiche, page 99 and Saskatoon Mixed Berry Jam, page 57.

3 oz cream cheese (90 g)
3 eggs
2 tbsp vanilla whey protein (25 mL)
1 tbsp vital wheat gluten (15 mL)
1 tbsp ground almonds (15 mL)
$^1/_4$ tsp vanilla extract (1 mL)
1 tsp olive oil (5 mL)

Yield: 9, 5" (13 cm) crepes
1 crepe
73.4 calories
4.7 g protein
5.6 g fat
0.8 g carbs

In cereal bowl with saucer for lid, microwave cream cheese 45 seconds. In medium bowl, using a wire whisk, whisk cream cheese and eggs until as smooth as possible. Add vanilla whey protein, vital wheat gluten, ground almonds and vanilla extract. Whisk vigorously until as smooth as possible. Do not worry about tiny lumps of cream cheese. These will disappear upon cooking.

In 5-inch (13 cm) nonstick frying pan (diameter of base), brushed with a tiny amount of olive oil, pour 2 tbsp (25 mL) of crepe batter. Tilt pan to coat with batter, using spoon to help spread it. Cook over medium heat. Flip crepe when edges are beginning to turn brown. Cook briefly on other side. Repeat.

COTTAGE CHEESE MINI PANCAKES

Tender ultra low-carb pancakes that are great for breakfast and also make super appetizers for serving fish mixtures or guacamole, page 12.

$^1/_2$ cup cottage cheese, (125 mL)
  lightly drained, if necessary
2 large eggs
2 tbsp vanilla whey protein (25 mL)
1 tbsp vital wheat gluten (15 mL)
1 tbsp ground almonds (15 mL)
1 tbsp olive oil, divided (15 mL)

Yield: 15 mini pancakes
1 pancake
22.9 calories
2.8 g protein
1.0 g fat
0.4 g carbs

In food processor or blender, combine cottage cheese, eggs, vanilla whey protein, vital wheat gluten and ground almonds; process.

In large, nonstick frying pan, spread a little olive oil. Drop pancake batter by 1 tablespoonfuls (15 mL) and cook until bubbles form. Turn over and cook briefly on other side. Repeat. (This recipe can easily be doubled)

SWEET COTTAGE CHEESE OMELET

Use small-curd cottage cheese and drain excess liquid.

1 egg
2 tbsp cottage cheese (25 mL)
$^1/_2$ tsp butter (2 mL)
Filling:
2 tbsp cottage cheese (25 mL)
1 tsp strawberry fruit spread (5 mL)

> **Yield:** 1 omelet
> 1 serving
> 136.9 calories
> 13.5 g protein
> 7.5 g fat
> **3.0 g carbs**

In cereal bowl, beat egg with fork. Stir in 2 tbsp (25 mL) cottage cheese. Melt butter in 5-inch (13 cm) nonstick frying pan (diameter of base of pan). Pour in egg mixture and cook until surface is set.

Filling: Place 2 tbsp (25 mL) cottage cheese and strawberry fruit spread on one side.

Fold omelet in half and serve.

Variation: Savory Cottage Cheese Omelet: Add 1 tsp (5 mL) chopped chives or green onion (green part). Omit strawberry fruit spread in filling. (**2.2 g Carbs**)

Helpful Hint: This recipe may easily be doubled to cook in a larger frying pan.

SAUSAGE-APPLE RING

Great for breakfast, served with scrambled eggs in the center.

2 lbs sausage meat (0.9 kg)
1 apple, peeled, cored and
  finely chopped
1 egg, slightly beaten
$^1/_2$ cup wheat bran (125 mL)
$^1/_4$ cup onion, chopped (50 mL)
$^1/_4$ cup whipping cream (50 mL)

> **Yield:** 12 servings
> 1 serving
> 335.1 calories
> 18.4 g protein
> 26.6 g fat
> **4.1 g carbs**

In large bowl, combine sausage meat, apple, egg, wheat bran, onion and whipping cream. Press into bundt pan lined with wax paper and bake in 350°F (180°C) oven 1 hour and 10 minutes. Drain excess fat. Unmold and serve filled with scrambled eggs.

JUMBO SOUR CREAM PANCAKES

Substantial, high in protein pancakes. Great with low-carb pancake syrup alongside sausage and scrambled eggs for breakfast, or topped with Crème Fraiche and fresh strawberries or blueberries.

2 eggs
1 cup sour cream (250 mL)
$^3/_4$ cup water (175 mL)
$^1/_2$ cup half-and-half cream (125 mL)
$^1/_2$ tsp vanilla extract (2 mL)
$2^1/_4$ cups Low-Carb Bake Mix, (550 mL)
  page 64
1 tbsp SPLENDA® Granular (15 mL)
2 tsp baking powder (10 mL)
1 tsp baking soda (5 mL)
$^1/_4$ tsp salt (1 mL)
1 tsp olive oil (5 mL)

Yield: 17 pancakes
1 pancake
106.6 calories
7.1 g protein
7.6 g fat
2.5 g carbs

In blender, combine eggs, sour cream, water, half-and-half cream, vanilla extract, Low-Carb Bake Mix, page 64, SPLENDA® Granular, baking powder, baking soda and salt. Blend, scraping down sides occasionally, until smooth.

Pour by $^1/_4$ cupfuls (50 mL) onto very lightly greased (use a pastry brush) 5-inch (13 cm) nonstick frying pan (diameter of base of pan) placed over medium heat. Cook until bubbles form and pancake sets. Flip and briefly cook other side. Repeat with remaining pancake batter, only greasing pan as required.

Helpful Hint: If desired, add fresh blueberries to the batter.

~~Bits & Bites~~
Using the Vital Ultimate Bake Mixes, page 66, instead of the Low-Carb Bake Mix, page 64 will mean the carbs will be somewhat higher, however, sometimes it is warranted in the case of breads, tortillas or pizza crusts, when a more robust "flour" is required for optimum results.

MICROWAVE MEATBALLS

These terrific meatballs converted my son, Jonathan. He did not like regular meatballs, until he had this lovely recipe sent from his ouma and oupa. Ouma and Oupa are my mother and father-in-law, Kay and Dr. Danie Eloff, who live in sunny Cape Town, South Africa, where they have retired.

18 oz extra lean ground beef (500 g)
1 egg
3 oz onion, grated* (90 g)
1 tbsp oat flour (15 mL)
1 tbsp low-carb Ketchup** (15 mL)
1 tbsp Worcestershire sauce (15 mL)
1¹/₂ tsp white vinegar (7 mL)
1 clove garlic, crushed
³/₄ tsp salt (3 mL)
¹/₄ tsp white pepper (1 mL)

Sauce:
2 tbsp low-carb Chutney*** (25 mL)
1 tbsp Worcestershire sauce (15 mL)
1 tbsp low-carb Ketchup (15 mL)
1 tbsp olive oil (15 mL)
1 tsp curry powder (5 mL)

Yield: 10 meatballs
1 meatball per serving
137.9 calories
10.5 g protein
9.5 g fat
1.6 g carbs

In large bowl, combine ground beef with egg, onion, oat flour, Low-Carb Ketchup, Worcestershire sauce, white vinegar, garlic, salt and pepper. Form into 10 meatballs. Place in 2-quart (2 L) microwaveable baking dish. Pour sauce over meatballs. Microwave uncovered on high power 10 minutes (1 minute per meatball).

Sauce: In small bowl, whisk together low-carb chutney, Worcestershire sauce, low-carb ketchup, olive oil and curry powder.

Helpful Hints: *Use 2 tbsp (25 mL) dehydrated onion (pour a little boiling water over it and let sit for a while), instead of grated onion, if desired. **I used Atkins Ketch-A-Tomato® for convenience, however, you may use Splenda Ketchup, page 89, *Splendid Low-Carbing*, if desired. ***You may either use a commercial product or low-carb apricot jam, or use Microwave Peach Chutney, page 102, *Splendid Low-Carbing*.

BEEF TACOS

Tender beef in wonderful, mildly spicy gravy for tacos.

2 lbs Beef Chuck Cross Rib (0.9 kg)
  Roast, trimmed of fat
2 cups tomato sauce (500 mL)
1 cup chopped onion (250 mL)
1, 4.5 oz can diced green chilies (127 mL)
1 clove garlic, minced
2 tsp oregano (10 mL)
1 $^1/_2$ tsp chili powder (7 mL)
1 tsp basil (5 mL)
$^1/_2$ tsp salt (2 mL)

Yield: 12 servings
1 serving (meat filling)
240.1 calories
25.2 g protein
12.8 g fat
3.7 g carbs

Cut roast into 7 thick slices. Place in crock-pot. In medium bowl, combine tomato sauce, onion, green chilies, garlic, oregano, chili powder, basil and salt. Pour over roast. Cook on high 5 hours (or on low 10 hours). Break up meat. Cook on low 3 more hours. Shred meat. Serve in low-carb tortillas, page 123, *Splendid Low-Carbing,* in Oat Tortillas, page 71 or in Cheese Tacos, page 35, topped with lettuce, salsa, cheese and sour cream.

Helpful Hint: I've also enjoyed this taco meat on an open-faced, one-egg omelet (prepared in 5-inch (13 cm) nonstick skillet), with all the above toppings.

~~Bits & Bites~~
Although one can use my cup-for-cup bake mixes instead of white flour, do not forget to adjust the liquid in your recipe by $^1/_4$ cup (50 mL) to $^1/_2$ cup (125 mL).

SWISS STEAK

This classic recipe was passed on to me by my friend, Jenita Davison, who lives in La Plata, MO. She lives in the country surrounded by lots of loving family, including 5 grandchildren!

2 lb round steak (0.9 kg)
$^1/_4$ cup Vital Oat Ultimate (50 mL)
  Bake Mix, page 66
1 tsp salt (5 mL)
$^1/_4$ tsp black pepper (1 mL)
2 tbsp olive oil (25 mL)
$^1/_2$ cup green pepper, sliced or (125 mL)
  chopped
$^1/_4$ cup onion, sliced or chopped (50 mL)
$^1/_4$ cup mushrooms, sliced, (50 mL)
  (optional)
1 cup tomato sauce (250 mL)
$^1/_4$ cup whipping cream (50 mL)
$^1/_4$ cup water (50 mL)
1 tsp SPLENDA® Granular (5 mL)

Yield: 6 servings	
1 serving	
252.0 calories	
37.2 g protein	
8.1 g fat	
5.0 g carbs	

Cut steak into serving size pieces. In small bowl, combine Vital Oat Ultimate Bake Mix, page 66, salt and black pepper. Sift bake mixture over meat and pound into steak with a meat mallet. Turn and repeat. In large electric frying pan, in hot olive oil, brown steak on both sides. Add green pepper and onion, cooking until vegetables are almost tender. Add mushrooms, if using. Add tomato sauce, whipping cream, water and SPLENDA® Granular. Cover and cook on low $1^1/_2$ hours, or until tender. Add water, if necessary.

~~Bits & Bites~~
I've switched from using natural whey protein powder (plain flavor) to vanilla whey protein powder, even for all of my savory applications as well, when used in the Low-Carb Bake Mix, Biskmix™, etc.

MEXICAN CROCK-POT PORK

Very simple, but very tasty, tender pork. This is mildly spicy.

3.5 lbs pork loin chops, (1.6 kg)
  center cut, boneless
1½ cups chopped onion (375 mL)
2 garlic cloves, crushed
1½ cups tomato sauce (375 mL)
2 tbsp white vinegar (25 mL)
2 tbsp Worcestershire sauce (25 mL)
2 tsp ground cumin (10 mL)
2 tsp chili powder (10 mL)
1 tsp basil (5 mL)
1 tsp paprika (5 mL)
½ tsp crushed red pepper (2 mL)
½ tsp black pepper (2 mL)
¼ tsp hot cayenne pepper (1 mL)
½ tsp Thickening Agent, page 62 (2 mL)

Yield: 8 servings
1 serving
402.0 calories
43.1 g protein
21.1 g fat
7.2 g carbs

Dice pork chops and place in crock-pot over onion and garlic. In medium bowl, combine tomato sauce, white vinegar, Worcestershire sauce, cumin, chili powder, basil, paprika, crushed red pepper, black pepper and cayenne pepper. Stir to combine well. Pour over pork.

Cook over low heat 7 to 8 hours. After 4 hours stir in Thickening Agent, page 62 and continue to cook another 3 to 4 hours.

~~Bits & Bites~~

Sucralose, created from ordinary sugar by changing the sugar molecule into something the body does not recognize, has no carbohydrates or calories. We are all just waiting for liquid SPLENDA® to be made freely available.

HAM WITH CHUTNEY GLAZE

Excellent glaze. Easy instructions for cooking ham.

9 lb cooked ham (bone-in) (4 kg)
Chutney Glaze:
Microwave Peach Chutney,
  page 102, *Splendid Low-Carbing*
$^1/_4$ cup Maple Syrup, (50 mL)
  page 172, *Splendid Low-Carbing,*
  OR a commercial product
$2^1/_2$ tsp prepared mustard (12 mL)

Yield: 25 servings
1 serving
171.4 calories
21.6 g protein
7.4 g fat
4.3 g carbs

Place ham in large, shallow roasting pan. Insert meat thermometer, being careful not to touch bone. Bake in 325°F (160°C) oven approximately $2^1/_2$ hours, or until meat thermometer reaches 150°F (66°C). Brush ham with some of chutney glaze in last 20 minutes. Reserve remaining chutney for serving with slices of ham. Remove ham from oven and let it rest 20 minutes before slicing.

Chutney Glaze: In blender, combine Microwave Peach Chutney, page 102, *Splendid Low-Carbing*, and Maple Syrup, page 172, *Splendid Low-Carbing* and mustard. Blend until smooth.

Helpful Hint: Since ham is generally very salty, slice thinly to prevent too much water retention.

INDONESIAN ROAST PORK

Rich gravy to go with your crock-pot roast.

5 lb pork shoulder roast (2.2 kg)
$^1/_2$ cup water (125 mL)
$^1/_3$ cup soy sauce (75 mL)
$^1/_4$ cup SPLENDA® Granular (50 mL)
1 tbsp instant chicken stock mix (15 mL)
1 tsp crushed garlic (5 mL)
$^1/_4$ tsp molasses, (optional) (1 mL)
1 tsp Thickening Agent, page 62 (5 mL)

Yield: 10 servings
1 serving
368.5 calories
46.2 g protein
17.6 g fat
3.1 g carbs

Place roast in crock-pot. In small bowl, combine water, soy sauce, SPLENDA® Granular, instant chicken stock mix, garlic and molasses, if using. Pour over roast. Cook on low heat 6 hours. Remove roast and slice thinly. Keep warm in covered dish in low oven. Turn crock-pot to high heat. Add Thickening Agent, page 62 and whisk until gravy has thickened. Serve roast pork slices with gravy.

BISKMIX™ MEXICAN PIE
Very tasty and such fun to assemble.

2 lbs lean ground beef (0.9 kg)
$^1/_2$ cup chopped onion (125 mL)
Taco Mix – recipe follows
$^3/_4$ cup water (175 mL)
2, 4.5 oz cans green chilies, (127 mL)
  (diced)
4 eggs, fork beaten
$1^1/_2$ cups half-and-half cream (375 mL)
$1^1/_3$ cups Biskmix™, page 65 (325 mL)
$1^1/_2$ cups Monterey Jack cheese, divided (375 mL)

Yield: 8 servings per pie	
1 serving	
489.7 calories	
33.1 g protein	
36.4 g fat	
5.9 g carbs	

Optional fixings:
Salsa
Sour cream
Taco Mix:
$^1/_4$ cup dehydrated onion flakes, optional (50 mL)
4 tsp ground cumin (20 mL)
$1^1/_2$ tsp hot chili powder (7 mL)
1 tsp salt (5 mL)
1 tsp garlic powder (5 mL)
$^1/_4$ tsp Thickening Agent, page 62 (1 mL)

In electric frying pan, cook ground beef and onion to brown; pour off fat. Stir in Taco Mix and water. Cook until dehydrated onion softens. Spread beef in two greased 9-inch (23 cm) glass pie dishes. Top with green chilies. In medium bowl whisk eggs, half-and-half cream and Biskmix™, page 65. Pour half this mixture over each pie. Bake in 400°F (200°C) oven 25 minutes. Sprinkle with cheese and bake 5 minutes longer. Cool 5 minutes. Serve with salsa and sour cream and a lovely, big salad, if desired.

Taco Mix: In small bowl, combine dehydrated onion flakes, cumin, hot chili powder, salt, garlic powder and Thickening Agent, page 62.

~~Bits & Bites~~
SPLENDA® Granular contains maltodextrin, a form of starch derived from corn. This is where the carbs come from (1 tsp = 0.5 g carbs).

HERB LAMB ROAST
Tender lamb with delicious gravy.

4 lb leg of lamb (1.8 kg)
$^1/_4$ cup olive oil (50 mL)
1 tbsp dried rosemary, crushed (15 mL)
2 tsp dried thyme, crushed (10 mL)
1 tsp seasoning salt (5 mL)
1 tsp crushed garlic (5 mL)
$^1/_4$ tsp black pepper (1 mL)

Yield: 10 servings	
1 serving	
467.0 calories	
33.4 g protein	
35.9 g fat	
0.6 g carbs	

Gravy:
Pan scrapings and 2 tbsp (25 mL) fat from roast
1 cup water (250 mL)
$^1/_2$ tsp Thickening Agent, page 62 (2 mL)
salt and pepper to taste

Cut slits all over lamb. Place in shallow roasting pan. In small bowl, combine olive oil, rosemary, thyme, seasoning salt, garlic and pepper. Rub herb-oil mixture over lamb, pushing some into pre-made slits.

Bake uncovered on center rack in 425°F (220°C) oven 45 minutes. Reduce temperature to 375°F (190°C) and cook 1 hour. Reduce heat to 350°F (180°C) and cook another hour, or until a meat thermometer (carefully inserted into roast to avoid touching bone) registers 175°F (79°C) for medium or 180°F (82°C) for well done. Serve sliced lamb with gravy.

Gravy: In small saucepan, combine pan scrapings, fat and water. Sprinkle Thickening agent over when gravy is scalding hot. Whisk until boiling and thickened. Add salt and pepper to taste. Blend in blender, if desired. If gravy is refrigerated it thickens even more. Skim off extra fat, if desired, before reheating and stir in a little water as necessary.

~~Bits & Bites~~
Flax seed is the world's richest source of Omega-3, an essential fatty acid.

POULTRY

CHICKEN AND BACON VEGGIE WRAP

Melted cheese, chicken, fresh veggies and my fabulous Creamy French Dressing.
This tortilla makes a great lunch with a diet soda or a Pink Lady, page 10.

1 large Oat Tortilla, page 71
  OR a commercial tortilla
2 oz cooked chicken (60 g)
1 slice bacon, cooked crisp
  and chopped
$^1/_3$ cup grated Cheddar cheese (75 mL)
$^1/_3$ cup shredded lettuce (75 mL)
3 tbsp sliced red onion (45 mL)
2 tbsp diced tomato (25 mL)
2 tbsp Creamy French Dressing*, (25 mL)
  page 59
few drops Tabasco sauce to taste

Yield: 1 serving
1 serving
411.3 calories
37.8 g protein
23.0 g fat
9.2 g carbs

Place tortilla open-faced on a dinner plate. In center place chicken, bacon and Cheddar cheese. Microwave 45 seconds, or until cheese has melted. Add lettuce, onion, tomato, Creamy French dressing, page 59 and Tabasco sauce (make sure these ingredients are ready and standing by). Fold tortilla over from opposite sides and gently turn over. Serve.

Helpful Hint: Ranch Dressing, page 61 may be used instead.

~~Bits & Bites~~
Raisins go further when you snip them in half and you may use less, because they do add quite a few carbs. The sweetness is spread more evenly in the baked goods and also in cooking.

CHICKEN FAJITA IN A MONTEREY TACO

The taco is made out of Monterey Jack cheese. It looks like a corn taco and has a milder flavor than a Cheddar cheese taco, thus it does not overpower the chicken. One or two of these tacos with a big salad is a very filling meal.

Chicken Fajita:
1 green or red pepper
$^1/_2$ cup onion (125 mL)
2 tbsp olive oil (25 mL)
5 cups diced cooked chicken (1.25 kg)
2 tsp Mrs Dash®Seasoning Blend (10 mL)
$1^1/_2$ tsp chili powder (7 mL)
$^1/_4$ tsp salt (1 mL)
$1^1/_3$ cups mild Salsa (325 mL)
Monterey Jack Cheese Taco:
1.5 oz grated Montery Jack Cheese (45 g)

Yield: 15 servings.
1 serving
207.6 calories
26.8 g protein
9.5 g fat
2.4 g carbs

In food processor with sharp S-blade, process red or green pepper and onion, until finely chopped. In electric frying pan or large skillet, in hot oil, cook green or red pepper and onion until turning tender. Add chicken, Mrs Dash Seasoning Blend, chili powder and salt. Stir-fry until chicken is hot. Add Salsa and stir to heat.

Monterey Jack Cheese Taco: Sprinkle cheese in bottom of 5-inch (13 cm) nonstick frying pan (diameter of base of pan). Cook over medium heat until turning light brown underneath. Flip cheese taco, using spatula and fork to help stabilize it while flipping. Cook briefly on the other side; about a minute or less. Place on dinner plate; fold over spatula (to keep it open) and fill with chicken mixture. Serve with a dollop sour cream on top, if desired.

Helpful Hint: This Chicken Fajita filling is also great in Oat Tortillas, page 71.

~~Bits & Bites~~

Vegetables are the mainstay of a low-carb diet. Eat a variety. Somehow overdoing carbohydrates from vegetables do way less damage than overdoing carbohydrates and calories from low-carb breads or desserts.

ITALIAN CHICKEN PIE

This is a good pie for an easy, quick supper using leftover chicken.

2½ cups cooked chicken (625 mL)
²/₃ cup Pizza Sauce, page 58 (150 mL)
¹/₃ cup green pepper, finely (75 mL)
  chopped.
1 cup grated Mozzarella, OR (250 mL)
  Cheddar cheese
²/₃ cup Biskmix™, page 65 (150 mL)
¹/₂ cup water (125 mL)
¹/₄ cup whipping cream (50 mL)
1 egg

Yield: 6/8 servings
1 serving
444.3/333.2 calories
46.7/35.0 g protein
25.6/19.2 g fat
4.5/3.3 g carbs

Cut chicken into bite size pieces. Spray 9-inch (23 cm) pie dish with nonstick cooking spray. In pie dish, combine chicken, Pizza Sauce, page 58 and green pepper. Spread out evenly. Cover with Mozzarella or Cheddar cheese.

In small bowl, whisk together Biskmix™, page 65, water, whipping cream and egg. Pour evenly over chicken mixture.

Bake in 450°F (230°C) oven 25 minutes. Allow to cool 5 minutes before serving.

CHICKEN GUACAMOLE MELT

Turns ordinary chicken breast into an elegant supper.

4 boneless, seasoned chicken breasts
4 slices bacon
¹/₂ cup Chunky Guacamole, (125 mL)
  page 12
4, 1.5 oz slices Mozzarella cheese (45 g)

Yield: 4 servings
1 serving
376.2 calories
46.9 g protein
18.6 g fat
3.4 g carbs

Wrap bacon around chicken breasts and place on broiler pan. Broil 10 minutes per side, or until juices of chicken run clear and no pink color remains. On each chicken breast, spread 2 tbsp (25 mL) Chunky Guacamole, page 12. Cover with slices of Mozzarella and broil until cheese has melted. Serve immediately.

CHICKEN MUSHROOM CASSEROLE

An easy, tasty supper casserole. This recipe is adapted from a recipe in "Cooking the Grey Way." My cousin, Leigh-Ann Taylor, used to teach at Grey Junior School in P.E., South Africa. I think there were 30 little boys in her classroom!! Leigh-Ann is the daughter of my aunt, Marie Richardson.

1 roasted chicken
12 oz fresh mushrooms (340 g)
1 tbsp butter (15 mL)
Curry Sauce:
1 cup whipping cream (250 mL)
6 tbsp bought low-carb ketchup, (90 mL)
  OR Splenda Ketchup, page 89,
  Splendid Low-Carbing
$^1/_4$ cup olive oil (50 mL)
2 tbsp white vinegar (25 mL)
1 tsp curry powder (5 mL)
1 tsp dry mustard (5 mL)
1 tsp SPLENDA® Granular (5 mL)
$^1/_2$ tsp salt (2 mL)
$^1/_8$ tsp black pepper (0.5 mL)
Topping:
$^1/_4$ cup sliced almonds, toasted (50 mL)
1 tbsp butter (15 mL)

Yield: 8 servings
1 serving
342.7 calories
30.1 g protein
26.9 g fat
3.9 g carbs

Debone chicken and cut into bite-size pieces. Place in 9 x 13-inch (23 x 33 cm) glass baking dish. In large frying pan, fry mushrooms in butter until softened. Layer over chicken.

Curry Sauce: In medium bowl, whisk together whipping cream, low-carb ketchup, olive oil, white vinegar, curry powder, dry mustard, SPLENDA® Granular, salt and pepper.

Pour sauce over chicken and mushroom layers.

Topping: Sprinkle almonds over casserole and dot with butter.

Bake in 350°F (180°C) oven 30 minutes.

~~Bits & Bites~~
Gluten flour is not the same as vital wheat gluten. I do not use the former.

FRIED CHICKEN

A great way to use up any of the leftover bake mixes. Serve with Corn Bread, page 63, if desired.

$^1/_3$ cup Vital Whole Wheat (75 mL)
  Ultimate Bake Mix, page 66, OR
  Bake mix of choice
1 tsp seasoning salt (5 mL)
1 tsp Mrs Dash® Seasoning Blend (5 mL)
$^1/_4$ tsp black pepper (1 mL)
1 egg
1 tbsp water (15 mL)
5 chicken legs (skin on, back attached)
2 tbsp olive oil (25 mL)

Yield: 5 servings	
1 serving	
356.2 calories	
43.0 g protein	
18.3 g fat	
2.3 g carbs	

In small bowl combine Vital Whole Wheat Ultimate Bake Mix, page 66 or Bake Mix of choice, seasoning salt, Mrs. Dash® Seasoning Blend and black pepper. Spread mixture on dinner plate.

In medium bowl, beat egg with fork and whisk in water. Dip chicken legs in egg wash and then roll in dry mixture on dinner plate. In large, nonstick skillet, such as an electric frying pan, fry chicken in olive oil on both sides, turning occasionally, about 25 to 30 minutes, depending on thickness. Chicken tests done when no longer pink inside and juices run clear. Cook half the chicken at a time in half the olive oil.

Helpful Hint: Use your own seasoning ideas, if desired.

~~Bits & Bites~~
I used super gluten (80%) in my recipes, however, usually 75% vital wheat gluten will be fine.

MEXICAN CHICKEN CASSEROLE
Delicious served with Chunky Guacamole, page 12.

1 lb cooked chicken, diced (0.454 kg)
1, 14-oz can sliced mushrooms, (284 mL)
 drained
4.5 oz can green chilies (127 mL)
1 tbsp chicken bouillon powder (15 mL)
$^1/_2$ medium onion
$^1/_2$ green pepper
2 tsp olive oil (10 mL)
2 tsp ground cumin (10 mL)
1 tsp chili powder (5 mL)
$^1/_2$ tsp black pepper (2 mL)
$^1/_2$ tsp onion salt (2 mL)
$^1/_2$ tsp garlic powder (2 mL)
1 cup tomato sauce (250 mL)
1 cup water (250 mL)
$^1/_4$ cup tomato paste (50 mL)
1 cup grated Cheddar cheese (250 mL)

> *Yield:* 6 servings
> 1 serving
> 185.8 calories
> 23.6 g protein
> 6.1 g fat
> *6.5 g carbs*

In 9 x 13-inch (2 L) glass baking dish, combine chicken, mushrooms, green chilies and chicken bouillon powder. In food processor, using S-Blade, process onion and green pepper until finely chopped.

In frying pan in olive oil, stir-fry onion and green pepper until tender. Stir in ground cumin, chili powder, black pepper, onion salt and garlic powder. In small bowl, whisk together tomato sauce, water and tomato paste. Add to vegetables and then add this vegetable mixture to chicken and mushrooms. Combine well. Sprinkle Cheddar cheese over top.

Bake in 350°F (180°C) oven 40 minutes, or until hot and bubbly. Serve with a dollop sour cream, if desired.

~~Bits & Bites~~
Low-carb baking does take some getting used to, however, over time one comes to prefer it. One loses the taste for sickly-sweet foods.

CHICKEN BROCCOLI CASSEROLE

A lovely recipe from my Aunt, Marie Richardson, who lives in British Columbia, Canada. She is a great cook, but best of all she is a wonderful aunt to me. This delicious casserole looks pretty as well. Great company fare!

1 cooked chicken
1 lb fresh broccoli (454 g)
2 tbsp fresh lemon juice (25 mL)
Condensed Cream of Mushroom Soup*,
 page 15
1 cup mayonnaise (250 mL)
1 tsp curry powder (5 mL)
$^1/_2$ tsp Thickening Agent, page 62 (2 mL)
$^1/_4$ tsp salt (1 mL)
1 cup grated cheese, Cheddar, OR (250 mL)
 Monterey Jack cheese
$^1/_4$ cup toasted, sliced almonds (50 mL)

Yield: 6/8 servings
1 serving
487.7/365.8 calories
10.0/7.5 g protein
47.3/35.4 g fat
6.2/4.6 g carbs

Debone chicken and place in greased 9 x 13-inch (23 x 33 cm) glass baking dish. In large saucepan, add broccoli to boiling, salted water and boil 5 minutes. Drain broccoli and layer over chicken. Sprinkle lemon juice over broccoli and chicken.

In medium bowl, combine Condensed Cream of Mushroom Soup, page 15, mayonnaise, curry powder, Thickening Agent, page 62 and salt. Spread over top of casserole. Sprinkle with cheese and top with almonds.

Bake in 350°F (180°C) oven 20 to 30 minutes, or until casserole is hot. Serve immediately.

Helpful Hints: For convenience, this casserole may be made ahead of time, covered and refrigerated until time to bake it.

* To reduce fat and calories, nonfat sour cream may be used in the mushroom soup and use light mayonnaise; however, the carbs will increase about 2 grams per serving.

~~Bits & Bites~~
Some of us get to the point where we can take or leave bread. Believe me, it used to be the mainstay of my diet, but now I can take it or leave it. It is possible! Now sweet treats for me are a different matter! I could not easily live without them as I seem to have an incurable sweet tooth.

WESTERN CHINESE

CAULI-FRIED RICE

This is my version of Chinese-fried rice using grated cauliflower. The color resembles golden brown rice. The cauliflower becomes denatured and hardly recognizable. It's delicious, especially freshly made.

$^1/_4$ cup Healthy Butter, page 53, (50 mL)
  Splendid Low-Carbing for Life, Vol-1
2 cloves garlic, crushed
1 green onion, chopped
6 cups cauliflower florets, (1.5 L)
  grated (about 1 medium head cauliflower)
2 tbsp soy sauce (25 mL)
$^1/_2$ tsp seasoning salt (2 mL)
2 eggs, fork beaten

Yield: 6 servings
1 serving
121.7 calories
4.4 g protein
9.6 g fat
4.3 g carbs

In electric frying pan or wok, melt Healthy Butter, page 53, *Splendid Low-Carbing for Life, Vol-1*. Add garlic and green onion. Cook briefly. Add grated cauliflower and stir-fry 2 minutes. Stir in soy sauce and sprinkle seasoning salt overall. Stir-fry another 3 minutes; push aside. Add eggs and scramble in one corner of pan. Stir into cauli-rice another minute, or until cauli-rice is tender.

Variation: Add small pieces cooked chicken or pork to cauli-rice.

Helpful Hint: Food processor grates cauliflower in no time flat!

~~Bits & Bites~~
Could you go back to low-fat ice cream and nonfat sour cream, low-fat brownies, etc? I know I couldn't. I think I have become spoiled on my low-carb diet.

GINGER SHRIMP AND VEGETABLES

Even my picky sons ate this entrée. The trick is to have all the ingredients handy and the vegetables already prepared before beginning.

1 lb shrimp, peeled and (0.454 kg) deveined
2 tbsp olive oil, divided (25 mL)
$^1/_2$ tsp crushed garlic (2 mL)
8 oz sliced water chestnuts (227 g)
4 green onions, chopped
$^1/_2$ red pepper, sliced in short strips
$^1/_2$ green pepper, sliced in short strips
$^1/_4$ cup water (50 mL)
2 tbsp soy sauce (25 mL)
$^1/_2$ tsp instant chicken stock mix (2 mL)
2 tbsp fresh minced ginger (25 mL)
$^1/_2$ tsp Thickening Agent, page 62 (2 mL)

Yield: 4 servings
1 serving
228.2 calories
24.2 g protein
9.1 g fat
7.9 g carbs

In 1 tbsp (15 mL) oil in wok, stir-fry shrimp 2 minutes. Transfer to plate. Pour off liquid in wok. Add remaining tablespoon (15 mL) oil to wok. Add garlic. Stir-fry 20 seconds. Add water chestnuts, green onions, red and green peppers, water, soy sauce and instant chicken stock mix. Stir-fry 3 minutes.

Return shrimp to wok with ginger and Thickening Agent, page 62. Stir-fry until sauce thickens and mixture is heated through.

~~Bits & Bites~~

When I first started low-carbing in 1999, cooking and baking, in particular, was a huge challenge for me, and there were no low-carb cookbooks out there with desserts, breads and baking in them that satisfied me. I really felt the need to pioneer a new path to baking low-carb, and finally these days thanks to the Lord's help, I find cooking and baking low-carb a wonderful joy and an outlet for my creativity.

SESAME CHICKEN IN LEMON SAUCE

A delicious entrée to add to another like ginger beef and a side of stir-fried vegetables and faux Chinese fried rice for dinner!

2.2 lb chicken breasts, (1 kg)
  cut into cubes
Light Crispy Batter:
3 eggs
$^2/_3$ cup Low-Carb Bake Mix, (150 mL)
  page 64
$^1/_4$ cup sesame seeds (50 mL)
6 tbsp water (90 mL)
2 tbsp wheat bran* (25 mL)
$^1/_2$ tsp salt (2 mL)
Buttery Lemon Sauce:
1 cup SPLENDA® Granular (250 mL)
$^1/_2$ cup butter (125 mL)
$^1/_4$ cup water (50 mL)
$^1/_4$ cup fresh lemon juice (50 mL)
1 egg yolk
2 tsp grated lemon peel (10 mL)
$^1/_2$ tsp Thickening Agent, page 62 (2 mL)

Yield: 6/8 servings
1 serving
477.4/358.1 calories
47.1/35.3 g protein
28.0/21.0 g fat
7.4/5.6 g carbs

Light Crispy Batter: In medium bowl, whisk eggs with wire whisk. Add Low-Carb Bake Mix, page 64, sesame seeds, water, wheat bran and salt. Whisk until well combined. Using tongs, dip chicken in batter and carefully place in hot oil at 350°F (180°C) in deep fat fryer, with basket already in place (otherwise batter sticks more). Cook until batter is golden brown. Remove basket and using a dinner knife, dislodge chicken from basket. Repeat. If batter becomes scant, see helpful hints below. Keep chicken warm and covered in a dish in low oven. Add Buttery Lemon Sauce just before serving.

Buttery Lemon Sauce: In double boiler, combine SPLENDA® Granular, butter, water, lemon juice, egg yolk, lemon peel and Thickening Agent, page 62. When butter has melted, whisk until sauce has thickened.

Helpful Hints: Calories and fat will be higher than shown due to batter absorbing some oil. If batter is running low and there is more chicken to dip, whisk in another egg and 1 tbsp (15 mL) Low-Carb Bake Mix, page 64 and a little water, if necessary. This will help the batter go further. *If desired, omit wheat bran and use only $^1/_4$ cup (50 mL) water, adding up to 2 tbsp (25 mL) water later, if batter becomes too thick.

GINGER BEEF

A favorite in our family. Calories will be higher due to absorption of oil.

2 lbs round steak, thinly sliced (0.9 kg)
  across the grain
Marinade:
$^1/_4$ cup soy sauce (50 mL)
6 tsp ground ginger (30 mL)
2 tsp SPLENDA® Granular (10 mL)
$^1/_2$ tsp Thickening Agent, page 62 (2 mL)
Batter:
4 extra large eggs
4 oz regular cream cheese (125 g)
$^1/_4$ cup oat flour (50 mL)
$^1/_4$ cup vital wheat gluten (50 mL)
2 tbsp wheat bran (25 mL)
Sweet-Sour Sauce:
$^3/_4$ cup white vinegar (175 mL)
$^3/_4$ cup Da Vinci® Sugar Free Pineapple Syrup* (175 mL)
$^1/_2$ cup water (125 mL)
$^1/_2$ cup SPLENDA® Granular (125 mL)
$^1/_4$ cup cooking sherry (50 mL)
2 tbsp soy sauce (25 mL)
1 tbsp tomato paste (15 mL)
$1^1/_4$ tsp Thickening Agent, page 62 (6 mL)

Yield: 8 servings	
1 serving	
340.2 calories	
42.4 g protein	
15.1 g fat	
8.4 g carbs	

Prepare steak and place in medium bowl. Pour marinade over sliced steak and marinate at room temperature one hour.

Marinade: In small bowl, combine soy sauce, ginger, SPLENDA® Granular and Thickening Agent, page 62.

Batter: In blender, combine eggs, cream cheese, oat flour, vital wheat gluten and wheat bran; blend. Pour into medium bowl.

Sweet-Sour Sauce: In saucepan, combine white vinegar, Da Vinci® Sugar Free Pineapple Syrup (*or pineapple extract, water and sweetener to taste), water, SPLENDA® Granular, sherry, soy sauce, tomato paste and Thickening Agent, page 62. Cook until thickened.

Using metal tongs, dip beef in batter, then carefully lower strips into oil in deep fryer (remove basket) and fry until lightly browned underneath, flip with fork and fry until golden brown all over. Keep beef covered and warm in dish in low oven and pour Sweet-Sour Sauce over meat when ready to serve.

CANTONESE ROAST PORK

An easy way to roast pork tenderloin or a pork center cut roast, giving it a Chinese flavor. Very tender.

3 lb pork tenderloin (1.4 kg)
2 tbsp olive oil (25 mL)
Marinade:
1 medium onion, very finely chopped
 (use food processor)
$^1/_3$ cup soy sauce (75 mL)
2 tbsp SPLENDA® Granular (25 mL)
1 tbsp dry sherry (15 mL)
2 tsp ground ginger (10 mL)
1 tsp salt (5 mL)

Yield: 10 servings
1 serving
276.7 calories
28.5 g protein
8.7 g fat
5.9 g carbs

Cut pork tenderloin into chunks about 1.5 inches (4 cm) thick (like a filet mignon steak) and about 4 to 6-inches (10 to 15 cm) long.

Marinade: In medium bowl, combine onion, soy sauce, SPLENDA® Granular, sherry, ginger and salt. Marinate pork 3 hours in refrigerator, turning at least once.

Remove pork from marinade, reserving marinade. Put pieces of pork in roasting pan in one layer. Stir olive oil into marinade. Baste pork with half marinade. Roast in 350°F (180°C) oven 15 minutes. Turn pork over and brush with remaining marinade, using it all. Roast pork another 15 minutes. Transfer to chopping board and cut chunks into thin strips before serving.

~~Bits & Bites~~

The nutritional analysis with each recipe portrays the net carbs, in other words, the fiber is already subtracted from the total carbohydrate value. In the nutritional analysis the carbohydrate total equals carbohydrate plus fiber. The fiber should not be counted as a carbohydrate as it does not act like one and is therefore allowed to be subtracted from the total carbohydrate value per serving. This is standard practice for folks following Atkins or Protein Power, two of the popular low-carb diets.

STIR-FRIED SESAME BROCCOLI

Sesame seeds and broccoli are a source of calcium, believe it or not!

1 lb fresh broccoli (0.454 kg)
2 tbsp olive oil (25 mL)
2 tbsp sesame seeds (25 mL)
1 tsp Mrs. Dash® Seasoning (5 mL)
  Blend (original)
$^1/_2$ tsp instant chicken stock mix (2 mL)
$^1/_2$ tsp SPLENDA® Granular (2 mL)

Yield: 4 servings	
1 serving	
93.8 calories	
3.5 g protein	
7.3 g fat	
3.8 g carbs	

Chop broccoli coarsely. Steam broccoli about 8 to 10 minutes, or until tender crisp. In wok, in olive oil, stir-fry broccoli briefly with sesame seeds, Mrs. Dash® Seasoning Blend, instant chicken stock mix and SPLENDA® Granular.

COLORFUL VEGGIE MEDLEY STIR-FRY

Versatile stir-fry to accompany any meal, not just Chinese.

1 lb fresh asparagus (0.454 kg)
1 red onion
2 tbsp butter (25 mL)
1 yellow pepper, sliced thinly
1 red pepper, sliced thinly
Teriyaki Sauce, page 48

Yield: 8 servings	
1 serving	
64.2 calories	
2.2 g protein	
3.1 g fat	
7.0 g carbs	

Break off asparagus tough ends by bending stalk back, until it snaps. Cut asparagus into short, diagonal pieces. Set aside. Cut red onion into small, thin wedges.

To melted butter in wok, add asparagus and red onion. Stir-fry 5 minutes. Add yellow and red peppers. Stir-fry a further 3 minutes. Stir in Teriyaki Sauce, page 48. Stir-fry vegetables briefly until sauce thickens.

~~Bits & Bites~~
The delicious meal replacement shake in Splendid Low-Carbing for Life, Volume One, is very useful to help induce ketosis.

PINEAPPLE SWEET AND SOUR CHICKEN

*Delicious battered chicken chunks, deep fried and served in a sweet and sour
pineapple sauce. Calories and fat will be higher due to batter absorbing oil.*

$2^1/_2$ lbs chicken breast halves, (1.1 kg)
  cut into cubes (about 8 breasts)
2 tbsp soy sauce (25 mL)
$^1/_2$ tsp black pepper (2 mL)
Batter:
3 extra large eggs
3 oz regular cream cheese (90 g)
3 tbsp oat flour (45 mL)
3 tbsp vital wheat gluten (45 mL)
2 tbsp wheat bran (25 mL)
Sweet & Sour Sauce:
$^1/_2$ cup white vinegar (125 mL)
$^1/_2$ cup Da Vinci® Sugar Free (125 mL)
  Pineapple or Vanilla Syrup, OR pineapple extract, water & sweetener
$^1/_2$ cup water (125 mL)
$^1/_3$ cup SPLENDA® Granular (75 mL)
$^1/_3$ cup tomato paste (75 mL)
1 tsp soy sauce (5 mL)
1 tsp Thickening Agent, page 62 (5 mL)
$^1/_2$ cup pineapple tidbits, (125 mL)
  canned in juice, drained

> **Yield:** 8 servings
> 1 serving
> 264.4 calories
> 38.4 g protein
> 7.9 g fat
> ***7.4 g carbs***

In medium bowl, toss chicken with soy sauce and black pepper. Using tongs, dip
chicken in batter and deep fry in deep fryer (without basket). Drop chicken
carefully into hot oil at 350°F (180°C) to avoid splashing. Remove chicken with
slotted spoon when batter is golden brown. Place in covered dish in low oven.

Batter: In blender, combine eggs, cream cheese, oat flour, vital wheat gluten and
wheat bran; blend. Pour into medium bowl.

Sweet & Sour Sauce: In saucepan, combine vinegar, Da Vinci® Sugar Free
Pineapple or Vanilla Syrup, water, SPLENDA® Granular, tomato paste, soy
sauce and Thickening Agent, page 62. Bring to boil. Stir in pineapple tidbits.
Pour sauce over warm chicken, just before serving.

Variation: **Thicker Batter:** 4 eggs, 4 oz (125 g) cream cheese, $^1/_4$ cup (50 mL)
oat flour, $^1/_4$ cup (50 mL) vital wheat gluten and 2 tbsp (25 mL) wheat bran.
(***7.8 g Carbs***). See page 43 for ideas on making batter go further.

TERIYAKI STIR-FRIED VEGETABLES

Use your own favorite combination of vegetables, if desired.

2 tbsp olive oil (25 mL)
1 lb broccoli & cauliflower (0.45kg) florets
1 red pepper
1 orange or yellow pepper
1 can sliced water chestnuts (227 mL)
Teriyaki Sauce:
3 tbsp soy sauce (45 mL)
3 tbsp SPLENDA® Granular (45 mL)
3 tbsp water (45 mL)
1 tsp ground ginger (5 mL)
$^{1}/_{2}$ tsp garlic powder (2 mL)
$^{1}/_{4}$ tsp Thickening Agent, page 62 (1 mL)

Yield: 6 servings
1 serving
95.6 calories
2.8 g protein
4.9 g fat
7.2 g carbs

In Wok or large electric frying pan, in hot oil, stir-fry broccoli, cauliflower, red and orange or yellow peppers and water chestnuts, until tender-crisp, about 6 minutes. Stir in Teriyaki Sauce in last 2 minutes.

Teriyaki Sauce: In small bowl, combine soy sauce, SPLENDA® Granular, water, ginger, garlic powder and Thickening Agent, page 62.

STIR-FRIED GINGER VEGETABLES

3 tbsp olive or peanut oil (45 mL)
$^{1}/_{4}$ cup chopped fresh ginger, (50 mL) (very finely chopped)
4 cups sliced mushrooms (1 L)
5 green onions, chopped
$^{1}/_{2}$ cup chopped red pepper (125 mL)
$^{1}/_{2}$ cup chopped green pepper (125 mL)
$^{1}/_{4}$ cup soy sauce (50 mL)
2 tsp instant chicken stock mix (10 mL)
4 cups bean sprouts (1 L)
3 eggs, fork beaten

Yield: 8 servings
1 serving
109.8 calories
5.2 g protein
7.3 g fat
6.2 g carbs

To oil in wok, add fresh ginger; stir-fry 1 to 2 minutes, or until turning brown. Add mushrooms, green onions, red pepper and green pepper. Stir-fry 2 minutes. Add soy sauce and chicken stock mix. Stir-fry another 2 minutes. Add bean sprouts and stir-fry a further 2 minutes. Pour eggs over vegetable mixture, leave for a brief 30 seconds. Stir again and leave until eggs are creamy. Serve at once.

CHINESE-STYLE SHRIMP

Serve over Cauli-Fried Rice, page 41, if desired.

3 tbsp olive oil (45 mL)
1 tsp ground ginger (5 mL)
$^1/_2$ tsp crushed garlic (2 mL)
24 oz frozen salad shrimp, (680 g)
  thawed (cooked)
14 fl oz canned cut green beans, (398 mL)
  drained
1 can sliced water chestnuts, (227 mL)
  drained
2 tbsp water (25 mL)
2 tbsp soy sauce (25 mL)
1 tbsp dry cooking sherry (15 mL)
2 tsp instant chicken stock mix (10 mL)
2 tsp SPLENDA® Granular (10 mL)
$^1/_2$ tsp Thickening Agent, page 62 (2 mL)

Yield: 4 servings
1 serving
313.6 calories
35.8 g protein
13.3 g fat
6.7 g carbs

In wok in olive oil, heat ginger and garlic. Add shrimp and stir-fry 2 minutes. Add green beans and water chestnuts; stir-fry 2 minutes.

In small bowl, combine water, soy sauce, sherry, instant chicken stock mix, SPLENDA® Granular and Thickening Agent, page 62. Pour sauce over shrimp and vegetables. Stir-fry 2 minutes. Serve hot.

Helpful Hint: To thaw frozen shrimp: Rinse shrimp in colander over basin under cold, running water 5 minutes.

~~Bits & Bites~~
My ultimate bake mixes as well as my low-carb bake mix make substituting for white flour in your own favorite recipes a breeze. Low-carb baking can be lots of fun and will tend to bring out one's own creativity.

49

CHEESE-STUFFED ZUCCHINI

Looks appetizing with golden brown, molten cheese.

5 zucchini
salted water
2 eggs, fork beaten
1$\frac{1}{4}$ cups grated Cheddar cheese (300 mL)
$\frac{1}{2}$ cup ricotta cheese (125 mL)
1 tbsp dehydrated onion (15 mL)
2 tsp dried parsley (10 mL)
$\frac{1}{2}$ tsp Mrs. Dash® Garlic & Herb (2 mL)
 Seasoning Blend®
$\frac{1}{4}$ tsp salt (1 mL)
$\frac{1}{8}$ tsp white pepper (0.5 mL)

Yield: 10 servings
1 serving
101.1 calories
7.1 g protein
6.8 g fat
2.1 g carbs

Cut both ends of zucchini off. Cook in boiling, salted water 10 minutes, until firm, but tender. Remove. Cut in half lengthwise and scoop out pulp. Dice pulp coarsely. Place in large bowl. Invert zucchini shells over paper towels to drain.

To pulp, add eggs, Cheddar cheese, ricotta cheese, dehydrated onion, dried parsley, Mrs. Dash® Garlic & Herb Seasoning Blend, salt and pepper. Mix well. Fill each zucchini shell and arrange in lightly greased 9 x 13-inch (23 x 33 cm) glass baking dish. Bake uncovered in 350°F (180°C) oven 30 minutes. Place under broiler on middle oven rack until turning golden brown, about 3 to 4 minutes (set timer!).

~~Bits & Bites~~
If you're missing breads, Splendid Low-Carbing has many to choose from, however, one of my best breads is in More Splendid Low-Carbing.

FAUX BAKED POTATO

A little taste of the real thing with delicious fixings is guaranteed to chase away feelings of deprivation, while the rest of the family or guests enjoy regular baked or mashed potatoes.

1 medium baking potato
1 tsp butter or olive oil (5 mL)
$^1/_3$ cup Creamed Faux Mashed (75 mL)
  Potatoes, *More Splendid Low-Carbing*,
  page 55
2 tbsp grated Cheddar cheese (25 mL)
Optional Fixings:
Real bacon, chopped
Cheese bits, page 72
Chives, chopped
Optional Garnish:
Sour cream

Yield: 1 Faux Baked Potato
1 serving
164.2 calories
5.8 g protein
12.7 g fat
5.9 g carbs

Scrub potato skin really clean with potato scrubber. Dry with paper towel. Rub potato with butter or olive oil. Bake potato in 450°F (230°C) oven 45 minutes or until skin is crispy and inside is soft when tested with a sharp knife. Cut in half lengthwise. Scoop out potato pulp and fill each half with Creamed Faux Mashed Potatoes, *More Splendid Low-Carbing*, page 55.

Optional Fixings: Add optional fixings of choice, if using, and sprinkle with Cheddar cheese lastly. Place in oven again until cheese has melted and faux potato filling is hot.

Optional Garnish: Garnish with a small dollop of sour cream, if desired.

Helpful Hint: Typically, half a Faux Baked Potato is enough. (***3.0 g Carbs***)

~~Bits & Bites~~
I keep my bake mixes in labeled, transparent and airtight containers at room temperature.

CAULI-NUGGET CASSEROLE

This recipe is based on our friend, Margaret Wolf's, potato casserole that she brought over for us to enjoy one Christmas day. It was a total hit! The topping for the low-carb version of her dish is crunchy and very tasty indeed!

2.2 lb fresh cauliflower (1 kg)
Condensed Cream of Mushroom Soup,
    page 15
2 cups sour cream (500 mL)
1 cup grated Cheddar Cheese (250 mL)
$^1/_2$ cup chopped onion (125 mL)
2 tsp Mrs Dash® Seasoning (10 mL)
    Blend (Herb and Garlic)
$^3/_4$ tsp salt (3 mL)
$^1/_4$ tsp white pepper (1 mL)
2 tbsp butter, melted (25 mL)
Cheesy Almond Topping:
2 tsp butter (10 mL)
1 cup sliced almonds (250 mL)
$^1/_2$ cup grated Cheddar Cheese (125 mL)

Yield: 15 servings
1 serving
225.1 calories
8.1 g protein
18.8 g fat
6.2 g carbs

Chop cauliflower florets really tiny – about the size of two hash browns – like little nuggets of cauliflower florets. Steam cauliflower 30 minutes, or until tender.

In large bowl, combine cauliflower florets, Cream of Mushroom Soup, page 15, sour cream, Cheddar cheese, onion, Mrs Dash® Seasoning Blend, salt and pepper. Spread evenly in 9 x 13-inch (23 x 33 cm) glass baking dish. Sprinkle topping over top; distribute evenly. Drizzle with butter. Bake uncovered 40 minutes in 350°F (180°C) oven.

Cheesy Almond Topping: In skillet, melt butter and stir-fry almonds until turning brown. Remove from heat. Quickly stir in cheese.

Helpful Hints: This casserole lasts a whole week in the refrigerator; however, it may also be frozen in an airtight container. It will not be quite as good as freshly made, but almost.

~~Bits & Bites~~
Chocolate chips are most often sweetened with maltitol, however, now Carbsense.com has come out with semi-sweet chocolate chips sweetened with sucralose.

MAPLE PECAN SQUASH

A sweet, yummy, crusty squash side dish. Butternut squash is a little on the carby side, but a little goes a long way, as it is so tasty.

3 cups mashed Butternut (750 mL)
  Squash (about 1 large squash)
2 tbsp butter, melted (25 mL)
2 tbsp whipping cream (25 mL)
2 tbsp Ketogenics® Pancake (25 mL)
  Syrup, OR Maple Syrup, page 172,
  Splendid Low-Carbing
¼ tsp salt, OR to taste (1 mL)
¼ tsp ground nutmeg (1 mL)
⅓ cup coarsely chopped pecans (75 mL)
2 tbsp Ketogenics® Pancake Syrup, OR (25 mL)
  Maple Syrup, page 172, *Splendid Low-Carbing*

Yield: 8 servings
1 serving
97.3 calories
1.1 g protein
7.2 g fat
7.4 g carbs

In medium bowl, combine Butternut squash, butter, whipping cream, Ketogenics® Pancake Syrup, salt and nutmeg. Spread evenly in 9-inch (23 cm) glass pie dish.

In small bowl, combine pecans and Ketogenics® Pancake Syrup or Maple Syrup, page 172 *Splendid Low-Carbing*. Sprinkle over top of squash. Bake in 400°F (200°C) oven 30 minutes.

Helpful Hints: An easy way to cook the Butternut squash is to boil it. Firstly, cut squash in half lengthwise and remove seeds. In saucepan over medium heat, heat squash (cut side down) to boiling in 1 inch (2.5 cm) water. Reduce heat to low; cover and simmer 15 minutes or until pulp is soft.

~~Bits & Bites~~
Before making a cheesecake, leave eggs and cream cheese at room temperature for about 3 hours. If time is a factor, soften cream cheese in covered dish in microwave oven and place eggs in bowl of warm water.

BROCCOLI 'N CHEESE

Here's an easy way to make broccoli more special.

4 cups chopped broccoli (1 L)
4 eggs, fork beaten
1 container ricotta cheese (500 g)
2 cups grated Mozzarella cheese (500 mL)
  (or thinly sliced)
$^1/_2$ tsp salt (2 mL)

Yield: 10 servings
1 serving
185.3 calories
14.5 g protein
12.0 g fat
4.5 g carbs

Steam broccoli about 20 minutes. In large bowl, combine eggs, ricotta cheese, Mozzarella cheese and salt. Stir in broccoli. Pour into a 2-quart (2 L) casserole dish. Bake in 350°F (180°C) oven 55 minutes.

MEXICAN-STYLE GREEN BEANS

Medium salsa gives these green beans a mildly spicy flavor; however, mild salsa would be a better choice for those who prefer less spicy foods.

1 lb fresh green beans (0.454 kg)
1 cup water (250 mL)
$^1/_8$ tsp salt (0.5 mL)
$^3/_4$ cup medium, OR mild Salsa (175 mL)
$1^1/_4$ cups grated Cheddar cheese (300 mL)

Yield: 6/8 servings
1 serving
129.6/97.2 calories
8.2/6.2 g protein
8.0/6.0 g fat
6.4/4.8 g carbs

Cut green beans into 2-inch (5 cm) pieces and place in large saucepan. Add water and salt and bring to a boil. Reduce heat, cover and simmer 15 minutes, or until green beans are tender. Drain. Spread green beans in shallow 2-quart (2 L) casserole dish. Stir in Salsa. Sprinkle Cheddar cheese over top. Heat casserole in microwave oven until cheese has melted. Serve immediately.

~~Bits & Bites~~
Studies have proven low-carbing to be an effective way to lose weight and most often blood pressure comes down and blood work values improve.

CHEESY ZUCCHINI TOMATO BAKE

This vegetable casserole goes well with meat loaf or steak.

3 medium tomatoes
1 tsp Mrs. Dash® Seasoning (5 mL)
 Blend (original)
$^1/_4$ tsp salt (1 mL)
$^1/_8$ tsp black pepper (0.5 mL)
$^1/_2$ cup mayonnaise (125 mL)
1 cup thinly sliced zucchini (250 mL)
$1^1/_2$ cups grated Cheddar cheese, (375 mL)
 OR a mixture of Cheddar and
 Monterey Jack cheeses

> *Yield:* 8 servings
> 1 serving
> 203.9 calories
> 6.4 g protein
> 18.7 g fat
> *2.5 g carbs*

In shallow baking dish, arrange sliced tomatoes in 2 layers on bottom. In small bowl, combine Mrs Dash® Seasoning Blend, salt and pepper. Sprinkle over layers of tomato. Spread mayonnaise over tomatoes and top with zucchini. Sprinkle with cheese and bake uncovered in 450°F (230°C) oven 30 minutes, or until zucchini is tender.

COTTAGE FAUX MASHED POTATOES

A delightfully different spin on the usual mashed cauliflower recipes.

6 cups mashed cauliflower (1.5 L)
 (1 large head of cauliflower)
$1^1/_2$ cups 2% cottage cheese (375 mL)
$^1/_2$ cup sour cream (125 mL)
2 tbsp grated onion (25 mL)
1 tsp Mrs Dash® Seasoning Blend (5 mL)
 (Herb and Garlic flavor)
$^3/_4$ tsp salt, OR to taste (3 mL)
$^1/_4$ tsp white pepper (1 mL)
$^1/_4$ cup toasted, sliced almonds (50 mL)
1 tbsp butter, melted (15 mL)

> *Yield:* 10 servings
> 1 serving
> 91.0 calories
> 7.1 g protein
> 4.9 g fat
> *4.4 g carbs*

In large bowl, combine mashed cauliflower (without anything added), cottage cheese, sour cream, onion, Mrs Dash Seasoning Blend, salt and pepper. Sprinkle with almonds and drizzle with butter. Spread in lightly greased 9 x 13-inch (23 x 33 cm) glass baking dish. Bake uncovered in 350°F (180°C) oven 30 to 40 minutes until hot and bubbly.

MISCELLANEOUS

RASPBERRY LEMON JAM

A sweet-tart jam that we enjoy very much. It's got more flavor in our opinion than the no sugar added raspberry jams commercially available, in our opinion.

6 cups fresh raspberries (1.5 L)
3 cups SPLENDA® Granular (375 mL)
1 cup water (250 mL)
$^1/_4$ cup maltitol crystals, OR (50 mL)
  8 SPLENDA® packets
1 box No Sugar Needed Pectin (49 g)
  (Bernardin®)
1 tbsp lemon juice (15 mL)
1 tbsp grated lemon peel (15 mL)
$^1/_2$ tsp butter (2 mL)

Yield: 4$^1/_4$ cups (550 mL)
1 tsp (5 mL) per serving
5.0 calories
0.0 g protein
0.0 g fat
0.9 g carbs

In 9 x 13-inch (23 x 33 cm) glass baking dish, cover two 2-cup (500 mL) jars and one 1-cup (250 mL) jar, lids and rings, a large, long-handled spoon and a pair of tongs with boiling water to sterilize. In large, nonstick saucepan, place raspberries. Add SPLENDA® Granular, water, maltitol crystals or SPLENDA®, Bernardin® No Sugar Needed Pectin, lemon juice and lemon peel. Stir well. Bring to full rolling boil, stirring occasionally. Mash with potato masher. Add butter. Boil hard for 1 minute. Remove saucepan from heat. Skim off any foam with long-handled spoon.

Carefully pick up jar with tongs and tip water out into sink. Place jar on saucer and spoon hot jam to within $^1/_2$–inch (1 cm) of rim. Pick up lid with tongs; place on jar. Pick up ring with tongs and screw on jar tightly, using a clean dish towel. Let cool. Lid will pop loudly when it seals. Refrigerate up to 1 year or freeze for much longer storage.

Variations: **Blueberry Lemon Jam:** Use fresh blueberries or frozen unsweetened blueberries, thawed. (*1.2 g Carbs*)

Strawberry Lemon Jam: Use frozen, unsweetened strawberries, thawed. (*1.0 g Carbs*)

Helpful Hints: I counted half the total carbs in the maltitol crystals. For those who cannot tolerate maltitol even in tiny quantities, use the SPLENDA® packets.

SASKATOON MIXED BERRY JAM

This jam is one of our favorites! We have tons of Saskatoon berry bushes/trees in our backyard and in the surrounding forest.

4 cups Saskatoon berries, OR (1 L)
  blueberries
4 cups mixed berries (1 L)
  (raspberries, blackberries and
  Blueberries)
$1^1/_3$ cups water (325 mL)
$^1/_4$ cup lemon juice (50 mL)
$4^1/_2$ cups SPLENDA® Granular (1.125 L)
$^1/_4$ cup maltitol crystals, OR (50 mL)
  8 SPLENDA® packets
1 box Bernardin® No Sugar Needed Pectin (49 g)
1 tbsp grated lemon peel (15 mL)
*1 tsp Slimsweet®, OR (5 mL)
  $^1/_2$ cup SPLENDA® Granular (125 mL)
$^1/_2$ tsp butter (2 mL)

Yield: $6^1/_2$ cups (1.6 L)
1 tsp (5 mL) per serving
4.5 calories
0.0 g protein
0.0 g fat
1.0 g carbs

In 9 x 13-inch (23 x 33 cm) glass baking dish, cover three 2-cup (500 mL) jars and one 1-cup (250 mL) jar, lids and rings, a large, long-handled spoon and a pair of tongs with boiling water to sterilize. In large, nonstick saucepan, place Saskatoon berries and mixed berries. Add water, lemon juice, SPLENDA® Granular, maltitol crystals (or SPLENDA®), Bernardin® No Sugar Needed Pectin, lemon peel and Slimsweet® or SPLENDA® Granular. Stir well. Bring to full rolling boil, stirring occasionally. Using a potato masher, crush berries (Saskatoon berries will mostly remain uncrushed and thus keep their volume). Add butter. Boil hard for 1 minute. Remove saucepan from heat. Skim off any foam with long-handled spoon.

Carefully pick up jar with tongs, using a tight grip, and tip water out into sink. Place jar on saucer and spoon hot jam to within $^1/_2$–inch (1 cm) of rim. Pick up lid with tongs; place on jar. Pick up ring with tongs and screw on jar tightly, using a clean dish towel. Let cool. Lid will pop loudly when it seals. Refrigerate up to 1 year or freeze for much longer storage.

Helpful Hints: *Slimsweet information can be found at: (www.trimedica.com and www.iherb.com/slimsweet2.html). 1 tsp (5 mL) Slimsweet® sweetener (**5 g Carbs**) is the equivalent sweetness of $^1/_2$ cup (125 mL) SPLENDA® Granular (**12 g Carbs**). I count half the total carbs in the maltitol crystals.

PIZZA SAUCE

This easy pizza sauce gives your pizza an authentic taste.

2, 5.5 oz cans tomato paste (156 mL)
1 cup water (250 mL)
1 tbsp SPLENDA® Granular (15 mL)
1 tsp oregano (5 mL)
$^1/_2$ tsp basil (2 mL)
$^1/_4$ tsp onion salt (1 mL)
$^1/_4$ tsp black pepper (1 mL)
$^1/_8$ tsp garlic powder (0.5 mL)
$^1/_8$ tsp salt (0.5 mL)

Yield: 2 cups (500 mL)
1 tbsp (15 mL) per serving
8.6 calories
0.4 g protein
0.1 g fat
1.5 g carbs

In medium bowl, whisk together tomato paste, water, SPLENDA® Granular, oregano, basil, onion salt, black pepper, garlic powder and salt.

Use $^1/_2$ cup (125 mL) per pizza crust.

Helpful Hints: Freeze leftover sauce or only make half this recipe for 2 pizza crusts, page 69. This Pizza Sauce will keep about 2 weeks in the refrigerator. Italian Chicken Pie, page 36, also uses this sauce.

EASY PEACH BUTTER

This flavorful butter spreads wonderfully on hot waffles, pancakes or even muffins and loaves, low-carb bread, etc. It keeps a beautiful, smooth spreading consistency in the refrigerator. Use light-flavored olive oil in Healthy Butter.

$^1/_2$ cup Healthy Butter, page 53 (125 mL)
  Splendid Low-Carbing for Life (vol-1)
$^1/_2$ cup Peach Jam, page 91, (125 mL)
  Splendid Low-Carbing or store bought
2 tbsp SPLENDA® Granular (25 mL)
1 tsp lemon juice (5 mL)
$^1/_8$ tsp ground nutmeg, OR (0.5 mL)
  cinnamon, (optional)

Yield: 1 cup (250 mL)
1 tsp (5 mL) per serving
19.2 calories
0.0 g protein
1.9 g fat
0.5 g carbs

In food processor, process Healthy Butter, page 53, *Splendid Low-Carbing for Life (vol-l)*, Peach Jam, page 91, *Splendid Low-Carbing*, SPLENDA® Granular, lemon juice and nutmeg or cinnamon (if using).

SWEET 'N SPICY MUSTARD SAUCE

Delicious with baked ham or even hard-boiled eggs. Lovely on low-carb meat sandwiches and many other uses besides.

$^3/_4$ cup sour cream (175 mL)
$^1/_4$ cup mayonnaise (50 mL)
$^1/_4$ cup prepared mustard (50 mL)
$^1/_4$ cup SPLENDA® Granular (50 mL)
$^1/_2$ tsp hot pepper sauce (2 mL)

> **Yield:** $1^1/_4$ cups (300 mL)
> 1 tbsp (15 mL) per serving
> 35.9 calories
> 0.5 g protein
> 3.5 g fat
> **0.8 g carbs**

In medium bowl, combine sour cream, mayonnaise, prepared mustard, SPLENDA® Granular and hot pepper sauce.

CREAMY FRENCH DRESSING

Better than store bought, in my family's opinion.

$^2/_3$ cup onion wedges (150 mL)
$^1/_2$ cup SPLENDA® Granular (125 mL)
$^1/_2$ cup Low-Carb Ketchup* (125 mL)
  (I used Atkins Ketch-A-Tomato®)
$^1/_2$ cup mayonnaise (125 mL)
$^1/_4$ cup white vinegar (50 mL)
$^1/_4$ tsp white pepper (1 mL)
$^1/_8$ tsp salt (0.5 mL)
1 cup olive oil (250 mL)

> **Yield:** $2^3/_4$ cups (675 mL)
> 1 tbsp (15 mL) per serving
> 65.7 calories
> 0.1 g protein
> 6.9 g fat
> **0.7 g carbs**

In blender, combine onion, SPLENDA® Granular, Low-Carb Ketchup, mayonnaise, vinegar, white pepper and salt. Blend. Slowly add olive oil through lid, while whipping on lower speed, until well blended.

Helpful Hints: *Alternatively, use my Spicy California-style Dressing, page 89 of *Splendid Low-Carbing*. Creamy French Dressing lasts at a least a month in the refrigerator in sterile jam jars or other similar containers.

59

HONEY MUSTARD DRESSING

This delicious dressing is a favorite of mine. Double the recipe and use as a dip!

$^1/_4$ cup mayonnaise (50 mL)
2 tbsp Ketogenics® Pancake (25 mL)
  Syrup (zero carb)
1 tbsp mustard (15 mL)
$1^1/_2$ tsp lemon juice (7 mL)
1 tsp honey, OR imitation honey (5 mL)

> **Yield:** 3 servings
> 1 serv./about 2 tbsp (25 mL)
> 147.1 calories
> 0.5 g protein
> 15.0 g fat
> *2.9 g carbs*

In small bowl, whisk together mayonnaise, Ketogenics® Pancake Syrup, mustard, lemon juice and honey. Serve immediately or refrigerate for serving later.

MOLASSES SUBSTITUTE

Strict low-carbers may want to give this recipe a skip until maintenance.

$^1/_2$ cup Ketogenics® Pancake (125 mL)
  Syrup (sugar free, sweetened with
  Sucralose)
1 tbsp molasses (15 mL)

> **Yield:** 9 tbsp (135 mL)
> 1 tbsp (15 mL) per serving
> 5.7 calories
> 0.0 g protein
> 0.0 g fat
> *1.5 g carbs*

In small bowl, combine Ketogenics® Pancake Syrup and molasses. Microwave briefly to melt molasses and stir to combine. Use in recipes; refrigerate leftovers.

PUMPKIN PIE SPICE

Vary the spices a bit to suit your own taste. Recipe doubles easily.

4 tsp ground cinnamon (20 mL)
$2^1/_4$ tsp ground ginger (11 mL)
1 tsp ground allspice (5 mL)
1 tsp ground nutmeg (5 mL)

> **Yield:** about 3 tbsp (45 mL)
> 1 tsp (5 mL) per serving
> 7.3 calories
> 0.1 g protein
> 0.2 g fat
> *1.3 g carbs*

In small container, combine cinnamon, ginger, allspice and nutmeg. Replace lid and shake to combine well.

RANCH DRESSING

An all-time favorite.

1 cup mayonnaise (250 mL)
$^3/_4$ cup buttermilk (175 mL)
$^1/_2$ cup sour cream (125 mL)
1 tbsp grated Parmesan cheese (15 mL)
2 tsp dried parsley (10 mL)
$^1/_4$ tsp garlic powder (1 mL)
$^1/_4$ tsp salt (1 mL)
$^1/_4$ tsp black pepper (1 mL)

> **Yield:** $2^1/_3$ cups (575 mL)
> 1 tbsp (15 mL) per serving
> 51.2 calories
> 0.4 g protein
> 5.3 g fat
> **0.5 g carbs**

In medium bowl, whisk together mayonnaise, buttermilk, sour cream, Parmesan cheese, parsley, garlic powder, salt and pepper.

OVEN PEACH SYRUP

If you have many peaches on hand in danger of spoiling, this is a great recipe to quickly save them. It can be used for waffles or pancakes.

6 cups peeled, pitted peaches, (1.5 L)
  sliced
$1^1/_2$ cups water (375 mL)
$^1/_2$ cup SPLENDA® Granular (125 mL)
$^1/_4$ cup Imitation Honey* (50 mL)
2 tsp lemon juice (10 mL)

> **Yield:** $3^1/_4$ cups (300 mL)
> 1 tsp (5 mL) per serving
> 3.3 calories
> 0.0 g protein
> 0.0 g fat
> **0.7 g carbs**

In large saucepan, combine peaches and water. Bring to boil over medium heat and boil gently 25 minutes. Blend peaches and water in blender with SPLENDA® Granular, Imitation honey and lemon juice. Pour peach mixture into 2, 8-inch (20 cm) glass baking dishes. Bake uncovered in 325°F (160°C) oven $1^1/_2$ hours to 2 hours, or until peach syrup reaches desired thickness. Fill sterilized, canning jars. Refrigerate as soon as cool.

Helpful Hint: *Instead of Imitation Honey, use extra sweetener or replace $^1/_4$ cup (50 mL) of water and the honey with $^1/_2$ cup (125 mL) Da Vinci® Sugar Free Peach or Vanilla Syrup.

THICKENING AGENT

This is useful to use instead of pure cornstarch or flour in thickening sauces.

$8^1/_2$ tsp xanthan gum (42 mL)
$4^1/_2$ tsp guar gum (22 mL)
$2^1/_4$ tsp Arrowroot starch*, OR (11 mL)
  corn starch*

> **Yield:** $^1/_3$ cup (75 mL)
> 1 tsp (5 mL) per serving
> 1.5 calories
> 0.0 g protein
> 0.0 g fat
> *0.4 g carbs*

In small plastic container with lid, combine xanthan gum, guar gum and arrowroot starch or corn starch; seal. Store at room temperature.

Helpful Hints: Substitute Thickening Agent for cornstarch, using $^1/_4$ as much and substitute Thickening Agent for flour, using $^1/_8$ as much to achieve approximately the same results.

This Thickening Agent must be used in small quantities to avoid a "gummy" texture. For instance, do not use in quantities greater than $^1/_2$ tsp (2 mL) for thickening sauces for stir-fried vegetables.

You may use only guar gum or only xanthan gum, if one or the other is not available. Xanthan gum is preferable to guar gum.

*Arrowroot starch and cornstarch each have about 7 grams of carbohydrate per tablespoon (15 mL). I've recently discovered arrowroot powder and it seems to work really well in my Thickening Agent. Used alone, it requires $^1/_3$ the amount of flour required to thicken sauces, etc. Sprinkle 1 tsp (5 mL) Thickening Agent over $1^1/_2$ cups (375 mL) boiling or hot liquid and whisk vigorously with wire whisk until liquid thickens. The Thickening Agent seems to dissolve really well, when there is some fat in the liquid, such as butter or olive oil or the fat in a stew gravy, for instance. If Thickening Agent has not completely dissolved, it may be necessary to pour the liquid through a sieve or blend in a blender.

Vegetable gums have the unfortunate characteristic of reducing sweetness in recipes somewhat, therefore, sometimes less Thickening Agent or more sweetener will be required.

Thickening Agent is utilized frequently throughout this cookbook; however, if you would like the convenience of a commercial product, then use "ThickenThin not/Starch" by Expert Foods (expertfoods.com). Things come out more or less the same.

BREADS, BAKE MIXES & BAKING

CORN BREAD

Southern fried chicken and corn bread comes to mind! Best fresh and eaten within a couple of days. Warm in oven or microwave oven before serving.

1 ¹/₂ cups Low-Carb Bake Mix, (375 mL)
  page 64
¹/₂ cup cornmeal (125 mL)
3 tbsp SPLENDA® Granular (45 mL)
2 ¹/₂ tsp baking powder (12 mL)
¹/₂ tsp salt (2 mL)
1 tbsp butter (15 mL)
2 eggs, fork beaten
¹/₂ cup water (125 mL)
¹/₄ cup whipping cream (50 mL)
¹/₄ cup olive oil (50 mL)

Yield: 10 servings
1 serving
194.3 calories
8.5 g protein
14.4 g fat
7.5 g carbs

In medium bowl, combine Low-Carb Bake Mix, page 64, cornmeal, SPLENDA® Granular, baking powder and salt. Add butter to a 9-inch (23 cm) round cake pan. Place in 400°F (200°C) oven to melt (watch carefully as this occurs quickly).

Meanwhile in small bowl, whisk eggs, water, whipping cream and olive oil. Stir into dry ingredients, just until combined. Swirl butter in pan and brush up sides. Pour batter into cake pan and bake in oven 20 minutes, or until golden brown on top. Serve warm.

~~Bits & Bites~~

The number of convenience low-carb, commercial foods seem to be increasing daily. The FDA is requiring stricter labeling, which will help the consumer to make informed buying decisions.

SPLENDID LOW-CARB BAKE MIX™

This tasty bake mix guarantees a low-carb result in your baking. Regular sugar and white flour recipes will have carbs reduced by about 75% to 85% or more, if Low-Carb Bake Mix is substituted for white flour and SPLENDA® Granular is used to substitute for sugar and high-carb dairy is changed to low-carb, etc.

$1^2/_3$ cups ground almonds (400 mL)
$^2/_3$ cup vanilla whey protein* (150 mL)
$^2/_3$ cup vital wheat gluten (150 mL)
{I used 80%, however 75% will work well in most recipes. Bob's Red Mill vital wheat gluten (75%) is very good quality} *This recipe will be referred to as Low-Carb Bake Mix in recipes.*

> **Yield:** $3^1/_3$ cups (825 mL)
> $^1/_3$ cup (75 mL) per serving
> 162.9 calories
> 14.3 g protein
> 10.3 g fat
> **3.3 g carbs**

In large bowl, combine ground almonds, vanilla whey protein and vital wheat gluten. Use a large wooden spoon to stir and mix well. See Helpful Hints below for instructions on how to use this bake mix. Store in a closed container at room temperature. Shake container to ensure ingredients are combined well.

To use this bake mix: For every cup of flour in your recipe, replace with 1 cup (250 mL) of Low-Carb Bake Mix, PLUS 2 tbsp (25 mL). The aforementioned rules apply also to replacing any of the Ultimate Bake Mixes from my previous cookbooks (which are a cup-for-cup substitution for all-purpose flour) as well as Vital Ultimate Bake Mixes, page 66 with this bake mix.

Once again, always add liquid cautiously to your own recipes that you wish to de-carb. Sometimes as much as $^1/_2$ cup (125 mL) less wet ingredients (this includes ingredients such as butter, olive oil, applesauce, pumpkin, water, yogurt, sour cream, cream, etc.) will be required. Typically, most of the time, it is $^1/_4$ cup (50 mL) wet ingredients that will need to be omitted from your regular recipe.

Helpful Hints: If very slightly coarser ground almonds (still almond flour) are used, the total yield for this bake mix is $^1/_3$ cup (75 mL) more than the 3 cups (750 mL) one would expect. If one chooses to see the yield as 3 cups (750 mL), the carbs increase slightly to 3.7 g. I only recently understood why this occurs, however, the recipes will not be adversely affected as differences are very slight. *If the application for this bake mix is for savory baking, it is possible to replace vanilla whey protein powder with natural whey protein powder, if desired.

Ground hazelnuts or pecans may be used instead. This bake mix is useful for piecrusts, muffins, loaves, many cakes, cookies and squares, some cooking applications and it guarantees lower carbs as well.

BISKMIX™

This exciting low-carb biscuit mix can be used similarly to Bisquick® in many favorite recipes. Bisquick®, a favorite Betty Crocker product, is the trademark of General Mills.

$2^1/_4$ cups Low-Carb Bake Mix, (550 mL)
   page 64
$4^1/_2$ tsp baking powder (22 mL)
$^1/_2$ tsp salt (omit with salted butter) (2 mL)
$^1/_2$ cup unsalted, ice cold butter (125 mL)
   {4 oz (113 g)} (Note: important to
   really use that amount for correct yield)

Yield: $3^1/_2$ cups (875 mL)
$^1/_4$ cup (50 mL) Biskmix
138.2 calories
7.0 g protein
11.6 g fat
1.8 g carbs

In food processor bowl with sharp S-blade, combine Low-Carb Bake Mix, page 64, baking powder and salt. Add butter, cut into small pieces; process only until mixture is crumbly (you don't want a dough ball). Leftovers can be stored at room temperature in an airtight container for about a week and transferred to the refrigerator or freezer for longer storage. Weeks-old Biskmix™ might need a boost with a little extra baking powder. Baked goods are best fresh. Chilled or day-old baking is often better reheated either in the oven or microwave oven.

Easy instructions for substituting Biskmix™ in recipes requiring Bisquick®:
Replace each cup (250 mL) of Bisquick® with 1 cup (250 mL) Biskmix™ PLUS an extra $^1/_4$ cup (or 4 tbsp) (50 mL) and typically use 2 tbsp (25 mL) less fluid than indicated in the recipe per cup (250 mL) of Bisquick® that will be replaced.

For example, if your particular recipe requires 2 cups (500 mL) of Bisquick® and 1 cup (250 mL) of fluid, you'd need to use $2^1/_2$ cups (625 mL) Biskmix™, and $^3/_4$ cup (175 mL) fluid. Simple math!

{1 cup = 16 tbsp; $^3/_4$ cup = 12 tbsp; $^2/_3$ cup = 10 tbsp; $^1/_2$ cup = 8 tbsp; $^1/_3$ cup = 5 tbsp; $^1/_4$ cup = 4 tbsp; $^1/_8$ cup = 2 tbsp}

Sometimes, for convenience, it is possible to approximate the amount of Biskmix™ required {for example, instead of using 1 cup plus 14 tbsp (475 mL), use a full 2 cups (500 mL)} and adjust the fluid requirements accordingly. Experienced bakers will know what a cookie batter looks like versus a cake, loaf or muffin batter, etc. Use plain whey protein in Low-Carb Bake Mix for savory applications, if desired, however, I always use the vanilla whey protein.

To accurately measure Biskmix™: Spoon into measuring cup, then level top with a flat knife. Do not scoop it or pack it down.

VITAL ULTIMATE BAKE MIX

Substitute cup-for-cup for all-purpose flour. Regular sugar and white flour recipes will have carbs reduced by about 60 %, if SPLENDA® is used as well.

Vital Ultimate Bake Mix (with spelt):
1½ cups ground almonds, OR (375 mL)
 ground hazelnuts, pecans or walnuts
1 cup spelt, OR all-purpose, (250 mL)
 whole wheat pastry flour, OR
 oat flour* (last two have fewer carbs)
½ cup vital wheat gluten (125 mL)

Yield: 3 cups (750 mL)
¼ cup (50 mL)/serv. (spelt)
139.5 calories
8.2 g protein
8.0 g fat
8.4 g carbs

In medium bowl, combine ground almonds (hazelnuts, pecans or walnuts), spelt flour (all-purpose, whole wheat pastry or oat flour) and vital wheat gluten; stir well. Substitute cup-for-cup for all-purpose flour. With all bake mixes, add liquid in your own recipes very cautiously, withholding about ¼ cup (50 mL) to ½ cup (125 mL) and adding it as necessary. Usually recipes require the former amount.

Variations: *Vital Whole Wheat Ultimate Bake Mix:** (using the same formulation in main recipe, only with whole wheat pastry flour):
131.4 calories, 7.8 g protein, 7.9 g fat, **6.9 g carbs**.

Vital Oat Ultimate Bake Mix: (using the same formulation in main recipe, only with oat flour): 136.5 calories, 8.1 g protein, 8.3 g fat, **6.1 g carbs**.

Vital Ultimate Bake Mix (with all-purpose flour): I very rarely use this combination, but will choose to make the bake mix with spelt flour instead as in main recipe with nutritional analysis shown. It is useful for a very special occasion, delicate-textured cake or loaf or muffins, etc.
144.1 calories, 7.9 g protein, 7.9 g fat, **9.7 g carbs**.

Helpful Hints: The ground almonds, all-purpose flour and vital wheat gluten combination in Vital Ultimate Bake Mix is very similar to regular baking and often better, producing lovely, moist, delicate-textured baked goods and is particularly useful for cakes that require a tender crumb texture. Spelt flour (a complex carbohydrate flour, not biologically related to wheat flour, but with about the same carbohydrate content) will be almost as good in such instances.

Vital Ultimate Bake Mix may replace Low-Carb Bake Mix, page 64 in recipes. Just use 2 tbsp (25 mL) less Vital Ultimate Bake Mix per cup of Low-Carb Bake Mix. It may also replace cup-for-cup any of the other Ultimate Bake Mixes in my other cookbooks.

CHEDDAR BISCUITS

These are similar to the ever-popular Red Lobster® biscuits. I couldn't make up my mind with these biscuits, which are both awesome, so provided both recipes.

$2^1/_2$ cups Biskmix™, page 65 (625 mL)
$^1/_2$ tsp baking powder (2 mL)
$^1/_2$ cup grated Cheddar cheese (125 mL)
3 tbsp water (45 mL)
3 tbsp whipping cream (45 mL)
Garlic Butter:
$^1/_4$ cup salted butter, melted (50 mL)
$^1/_2$ tsp garlic powder (2 mL)

Yield: 9 biscuits
1 biscuit
242.4 calories
9.6 g protein
21.9 g fat
2.4 g carbs

In large bowl, combine Biskmix™, page 65 and baking powder. Stir in Cheddar cheese. Make well in center and pour in water and whipping cream. Using a wooden spoon, stir until soft dough forms. Beat with wooden spoon 30 seconds or so. Spoon onto greased cookie sheet by $^1/_4$ cupfuls (50 mL). Do not flatten (they will naturally spread out) – just scoop out with teaspoon and drop them. Bake 8 to 10 minutes in 450°F (230°C) oven or until turning brown.

Garlic Butter: In small bowl, combine melted butter and garlic powder. Brush* over tops of baked, hot biscuits and serve immediately.

Variation: **Cheddar Biscuit #2:** Substitute $3^1/_2$ cups (875 mL) Biskmix™ (the entire batch), page 65, $^1/_4$ tsp (1 mL) baking powder, $^2/_3$ cup (150 mL) Cheddar cheese, $^1/_3$ cup (75 mL) water and 3 tbsp (45 mL) whipping cream. Bake 8 to 10 minutes in 450°F (230°C) oven. Use same garlic butter to brush over hot biscuits. *Yield:* 12 biscuits. (231.8 calories; 9.8 g protein, 20.7 g fat, ***2.4 g carbs***)

Helpful Hints: *If you don't have a pastry brush, an unused, clean, soft paint brush (small or medium size) works very well, believe it or not!

If these biscuits are made ahead of time, reheat by placing biscuits directly on oven rack in 350°F (180°C) oven and heat 5 to 7 minutes.

These delicious Cheddar Biscuits are best served hot from the oven and would be excellent served with seafood to remind one of a fabulous dinner at Red Lobster®. Choose a fish and/or shellfish recipe from one of my cookbooks, if desired. No extra butter is required to spread on the biscuits. These biscuits may be frozen. Microwave 40 seconds and place directly on oven rack in 350°F (180°C) oven 5 to 7 minutes or until crisper.

ITALIAN FLATBREAD

Served warm out of the oven, this bread is great as a side with a good meal.

$2^1/_2$ cups Biskmix™, page 65 (625 mL)
$^1/_4$ cup hot water (50 mL)
2 tbsp butter, melted (25 mL)
$^1/_2$ cup grated Cheddar cheese (125 mL)
$^1/_4$ cup grated Monterey Jack (50 mL)
  cheese
2 tbsp grated Parmesan cheese (25 mL)
2 tsp dried parsley (10 mL)
1 tsp Mrs Dash® Seasoning blend (5 mL)
  (use garlic and herb, if desired)

Yield: 12 servings
1 serving
165.2 calories
8.1 g protein
14.2 g fat
1.9 g carbs

In medium bowl, combine Biskmix™, page 65 and hot water. Place dough on ungreased cookie sheet, cover with a piece of plastic wrap and press out evenly into an 8 x 11-inch (20 x 28 cm) rectangle. Brush melted butter over dough.

In small bowl, combine Cheddar cheese, Monterey Jack cheese, Parmesan cheese, parsley and Mrs Dash® Seasoning blend. Sprinkle over dough.

Bake in 450°F (230°C) oven 8 to 10 minutes, or until light golden brown. Serve warm.

Helpful Hints: To reheat refrigerated Italian Flatbread, microwave briefly or heat in moderate oven a few minutes.

I use the leftover 1 cup (250 mL) Biskmix™, by stirring in 1 tbsp (15 mL) water and also 1 cup (250 mL) Monterey Jack cheese. Spread into a smaller rectangle and bake as in above recipe. It is great served warm with low-carb peach jam. ***Yield:*** 6 servings. 166.4 calories, 9.5 g protein, 13.8 g fat, 1.7 g carbs.

~~Bits & Bites~~
Soy consumption should be minimal to zero for a person suffering from hypothyroidism or any type of thyroid disease. I have Hashimoto's Thyroiditis and I really try to avoid soy these days. This caution does not apply to fermented soy sauce, however, which can be consumed in moderation. I don't believe I have used soy flour or soy isolate since More Splendid Low-Carbing.

THIN 'N CRISPY PIZZA CRUST

Thin, crispy crust pizza is a favorite. My eldest son, Daniel, 20 years old, who is not fully into low-carbing said, "Mom, this tastes equivalent to high-carb pizza. In fact, I actually prefer yours to the ones with the thick, white flour crusts."

1 $^1/_3$ cups water (325 mL)
4 cups Vital Oat Ultimate (1 L)
 Bake Mix, page 66, OR use
 Whole wheat pastry flour in Bake Mix
 for about the same carbs
2 tbsp butter (25 mL)
2 tbsp skim, OR whole milk (25 mL)
 powder
1 tbsp sugar (food for yeast) (15 mL)
1 tbsp dry yeast (15 mL)
1 tsp salt (5 mL)
3 tbsp olive oil, or more to taste (45 mL)

Yield: 2 pizzas, 12 serv. ea.
1 serving
117.3 calories
5.7 g protein
8.2 g fat
4.4 g carbs

In bread pan, place water, Vital Oat Ultimate Bake Mix, page 66, butter, skim or whole milk powder, sugar (yeast completely consumes the sugar and forms carbon dioxide, which is what makes the bread rise), dry yeast and salt. Program bread machine to "dough" setting. Scrape sides of pan in the beginning, while it is mixing. Remove dough when ready and roll out on counter to fit a large pizza pan (larger than 12 inches (30 cm), preferably one with holes in it. Brush one side of dough with 2 tbsp (25 mL) olive oil and place that side down on pizza pan. If necessary, use small rolling pin or cylindrical object to further roll out dough. Bake in center of 425°F (200°C) oven 10 minutes. Remove and brush top of crust with remaining olive oil (use extra, if desired). Carefully loosen crust and flip using potholders. Bake another 5 minutes.

Cover with Pizza Sauce, page 58, add toppings, such as sliced wieners or ham and chopped bacon and Mozzarella, Cheddar and Parmesan Cheeses. Using Pizza Sauce, page 58, 4 wieners (sliced), 4 strips bacon (cooked and chopped) and 2 cups (500 mL) Mozzarella cheese on each pizza: (*6.7 g Carbs*). Reduce heat to 375°F (190°C) and bake 15 to 20 minutes, or until crust is crispy and brown underneath and cheese has melted. It may be necessary to cover or partially cover pizza lightly with foil if top crust is turning too brown.

Helpful Hints: It is easy to add interest to the above pizza topping suggestions, such as finely chopped red and green pepper, sliced mushrooms, chopped green onions, etc. Add your own meat fixings and toppings – be creative! It's possible to roll out remaining pizza crust, place on pizza pan or roll to fit a cookie sheet, cover with plastic wrap, refrigerate and bake the next day (even crispier!).

CHEDDAR CHEESE MUFFINS

These muffins are really special. They would be great for breakfast or teatime with low-carb apricot jam, page 91, Splendid Low-carbing (just substitute apricots for the peaches and nectarines).

2 eggs
$3^3/_4$ cups Biskmix™, page 65 (925 mL)
  (need to make 2 batches)
$1^1/_3$ cups grated Cheddar cheese (325 mL)
  (divided)
$^1/_2$ cup SPLENDA® Granular (125 mL)
$^1/_2$ cup water (125 mL)
$^1/_4$ cup whipping cream (50 mL)
3 tbsp olive oil (45 mL)

Yield: 12 muffins
1 per serving
287.3 calories
13.1 g protein
24.7 g fat
3.7 g carbs

In large bowl, whisk eggs. Stir in Biskmix™, page 65, 1 cup (250 mL) Cheddar cheese, SPLENDA® Granular, water, whipping cream and olive oil. Fill 12 muffin cups $^3/_4$ full. Sprinkle top of dough with remaining $^1/_3$ cup (75 mL) Cheddar cheese.

Bake in 400°F (200°C) oven 15 to 17 minutes. Remove from pan immediately. Serve warm. Microwave day-old muffins 15 seconds.

DUMPLINGS

Top off beef stew, page 30, More Splendid Low-Carbing with these dumplings.

$2^1/_2$ cups Biskmix™, page 65 (625 mL)
  (use natural whey protein in Low-Carb
  Bake Mix, page 64, if desired)
$^1/_8$ tsp salt (0.5 mL)
6 tbsp half-and-half cream (90 mL)

Yield: 8/10 servings
1 serving
186.1/148.9 calories
9.1/7.3 g protein
15.6/12.5 g fat
2.8/2.2 g carbs

In medium bowl, stir Biskmix™, page 65, salt and half-and-half cream together to form soft dough. Drop by large soup spoonfuls onto lightly simmering stew (hopefully onto something more solid than just pure liquid). Reduce heat to 325°F (160°C). Cook in roaster uncovered 10 minutes. Cover and cook another 10 minutes.

Helpful Hint: If desired, flavor Biskmix™, page 65 in recipe above with your own seasonings or 1 tsp (5 mL) Mrs Dash® Seasoning blend.

OAT TORTILLAS

This is so easy, although a bit time consuming, but what a tasty tortilla! Between rolling and cooking tortillas, I typically clean the kitchen, so that when all is said and done, the kitchen is spotless as well.

1$^1/_3$ cups water (325 mL)
4 cups Vital Oat Ultimate (1 L)
  Bake Mix, page 66, OR use
  Whole wheat pastry flour in Bake Mix
  For about the same carbs
2 tbsp butter (25 mL)
2 tbsp skim, OR whole milk (25 mL)
  powder
1 tbsp sugar (15 mL)
1 tbsp bread machine yeast (15 mL)
1 tsp salt (5 mL)

> *Yield:* 20 tortillas
> 1 tortilla per serving
> 122.8 calories
> 6.9 g protein
> 7.8 g fat
> *5.2 g carbs*

In bread pan, place water, Vital Oat Ultimate Bake Mix, page 66, butter, skim or whole milk powder, sugar (food for yeast – completely consumed), bread machine yeast and salt. Program bread machine to dough setting. Scrape sides of loaf pan, while it is mixing, to incorporate all the dough. Remove dough when cycle is done and cover with clean tea towel. Break off small balls. Each ball should weigh 1.5 oz (43 g). Roll each ball out very thinly on counter top between two pieces of wax paper, or dust counter top surface (if necessary) with a little Vital Oat Ultimate Bake Mix or whey protein powder or your choice of "flour" and roll out. Cover balls with clean tea towel. Roll out one ball at a time into a very thin circle, about 7 inches (18 cm) in diameter. Lift carefully with flat, hard spatula or knife. Place tortilla in dry, nonstick frying pan. Cook over medium heat until brown spots appear underneath, flip and cook other side briefly. Reduce heat slightly, if they are turning too brown. There will be minimal shrinkage, if any.

Helpful Hints: Keep covered and later store in a sealed plastic bag in refrigerator. These will keep about two weeks in the refrigerator. Microwave 15 to 30 seconds to reheat. For longer storage, freeze tortillas in sealed plastic bag.

~~Bits & Bites~~
Low-carb bars, chocolate, desserts and breads can slow weight loss in some people. It is actually wise to keep low-carb treats for the weekend.

GINGERBREAD MUFFINS

I like these brown gingerbread muffins plain or buttered and spread with a tiny amount of strawberry fruit spread.

1$^3/_4$ cups Low-Carb Bake Mix, (425 mL) page 64
1 tsp baking soda (5 mL)
1 tsp cinnamon (5 mL)
$^1/_2$ tsp ground ginger (2 mL)
$^1/_2$ tsp ground cloves (2 mL)
$^1/_4$ tsp ground nutmeg (1 mL)
$^1/_4$ tsp dry mustard (1 mL)
$^1/_4$ tsp salt (1 mL
1 extra-large egg
$^1/_2$ cup Molasses Substitute, page 60 (125 mL)
$^1/_3$ cup olive oil (75 mL)
$^1/_4$ cup boiling water (50 mL)

Yield: 10 muffins
1 muffin
164.0 calories
8.3 g protein
13.2 g fat
3.4 g carbs

In large bowl, combine Low-Carb Bake Mix, page 64, baking soda, cinnamon, ginger, cloves, nutmeg, dry mustard and salt. In small bowl, beat egg with fork. Stir in Molasses Substitute, page 60 and olive oil. Pour into well made in dry ingredients. Mix just until moistened. Add boiling water and mix until blended. Fill 10 greased muffin cups about half full. Bake 15 to 20 minutes in 350°F (180°C) oven, or until knife inserted in muffin comes out clean and tops are nicely browned. Cool in pan on wire rack.

EASY BISKMIX™ CRACKERS

Great for using up leftover Biskmix™, page 65. Overcooked the crackers? Crumble and use as "Cheese Bits" on casseroles or instead of bacon bits.

$^1/_2$ cup grated Cheddar cheese (125 mL)
$^1/_3$ cup Biskmix™, page 65 (75 mL)
2 tsp water (10 mL)

Yield: 2 servings
1 serving
211.6 calories
12.1 g protein
17.5 g fat
1.6 g carbs

In small bowl, combine Cheddar cheese, Biskmix™, page 65 and water. Place on greased dinner plate and using plastic wrap, press out dough to fill inside of plate. Microwave on high power 2 to 4 minutes until crisp.

ZUCCHINI RAISIN BRAN MUFFINS

Healthy, moist bran muffins to make a "regular" part of one's diet. These muffins smell incredibly good while baking.

1 1/2 cups Low-Carb Bake (375 mL)
  Mix, page 64
1 cup wheat bran (250 mL)
3 tbsp SPLENDA® Granular (45 mL)
2 tsp baking powder (10 mL)
1/4 tsp salt (1 mL)
1/4 cup water (50 mL)
1/4 cup whipping cream (50 mL)
1/4 cup olive oil (50 mL)
3 tbsp Ketogenics® Pancake Syrup, OR (45 mL)
  Maple Syrup, page 172, *Splendid Low-Carbing*
1 tsp molasses, optional (5 mL)
1 egg, fork beaten
1 cup grated zucchini (250 mL)
1/4 cup plump raisins, snipped in half, optional (50 mL)

Yield: 12 muffins
With/without raisins
150.1/139.9 calories
7.0/7.0 g protein
10.8/10.8 g fat
6.0/3.6 g carbs

In large mixing bowl, combine Low-Carb Bake Mix, page 64, wheat bran, SPLENDA® Granular, baking powder and salt. Make well in center. Pour in water, whipping cream, olive oil, Ketogenics® Pancake Syrup, molasses and egg; stir to mix. Stir in zucchini and raisins. Fill 12 greased muffin cups. Bake in 400°F (200°C) oven 15 to 20 minutes, or until knife inserted in muffins comes out clean.

~~Bits & Bites~~
Studies have proven almonds to be heart healthy and not to have adverse effects on weight loss. <u>www.almondsarein.com/health</u>

LEMON CRANBERRY MINI LOAVES

A blend of slightly tart and sweet, lemony flavors.

2 cups frozen cranberries (500 mL)
  (unsweetened)
2 tbsp SPLENDA® Granular (25 mL)
$^2/_3$ cup butter, softened (150 mL)
4 eggs
$1^1/_2$ cups SPLENDA® Granular (375 mL)
3 tbsp lemon juice (45 mL)
2 tbsp grated lemon peel (25 mL)
$3^1/_2$ cups Low-Carb Bake Mix, page 64 (875 mL)
2 tsp baking powder (10 mL)
$^1/_2$ tsp baking soda (2 mL)
$^1/_4$ tsp salt (1 mL)
$^2/_3$ cup water (150 mL)
$^1/_3$ cup whipping cream (75 mL)
1 cup finely chopped pecans or walnuts (250 mL)
Lemon Glaze:
6 tbsp SPLENDA® Granular (90 mL)
$^1/_4$ cup fresh lemon juice (50 mL)
$^1/_4$ tsp Thickening Agent, page 62 (1 mL)

Yield: 40 (10 x 4) servings
1 serving
111.8 calories
4.7 g protein
8.9 g fat
3.3 g carbs

In food processor with metal S-blade or in blender, process cranberries, using pulse button until cranberries are finely chopped. Stir in 2 tbsp (25 mL) SPLENDA® Granular. Set aside. In food processor with S-blade or in bowl with electric mixer, cream the butter. Add eggs, $1^1/_2$ cups (375 mL) SPLENDA® Granular, lemon juice, and lemon peel; process.

In medium bowl, combine Low-Carb Bake Mix, page 64, baking powder, baking soda and salt. Add to creamed mixture alternately with water and whipping cream; process just until combined. Stir in prepared cranberries and chopped pecans or walnuts. Scoop into 4 mini greased nonstick $5^3/_4$ x $3^1/_4$ x $2^1/_4$ inch (15 x 8 x 6 cm) loaf pans. Bake in 350°F (180°C) oven 40 minutes, or until knife inserted in center comes out clean. Invert loaves onto wire rack. Place right side up and brush warm loaves with Lemon Glaze.

Lemon Glaze: While loaves are baking, place SPLENDA® Granular, lemon juice and Thickening Agent in small saucepan and bring to boil, while whisking. Sieve, using spoon to push sauce through. Add yellow food coloring, if desired.

Helpful Hints: It is easy to cut ultra-thin slices of this loaf, if desired. These loaves freeze successfully. When cool, wrap in plastic wrap, then in foil. Freeze.

FROZEN DESSERTS & MISCELLANEOUS DESSERTS

CRANBERRY SLUSHIE

So refreshing and so few calories too! You can double this recipe.

6 oz frozen cranberries (170 g)
1¼ cups water (300 mL)
1 cup Da Vinci® Sugar Free (250 mL)
 Raspberry or Orange Syrup
½ cup SPLENDA® Granular (125 mL)

Yield: 4 servings
1 serving
25.9 calories
0.1 g protein
0.1 g fat
5.4 g carbs

In large saucepan, combine cranberries and water. Bring to boil. Boil 5 minutes. Remove from heat. Let cool slightly. Place sieve over a bowl. Add cranberries and pulverize them through the sieve, using a spoon underneath to remove any pulp. Stir Da Vinci® Sugar Free Raspberry or Orange Syrup and SPLENDA® Granular into Cranberry juice. Place bowl in freezer half an hour. Freeze cranberry mixture in ice cream maker until turning slushy.

Place slush in bowl in freezer. Place ice cream container in sink of hot water to remove remaining slush ice stuck to sides. This could take up to half an hour for it to loosen. Stir into rest of slush and serve (eat with a spoon).

Variation: **Da Vinci® Alternative:** Substitute sugar free Kool-Aid®, water and sweetener to taste.

~~Bits & Bites~~
Erythritol is a sugar alcohol that seems to be innocuous as far as causing digestive upset. It can be used in small quantities in combination with SPLENDA® Granular in some applications. It does have a slight "cooling" effect on the taste buds; however, this is minimized by using small amounts.

STRAWBERRY SHERBET

Excellent treat, especially on a hot, sunny day.

3 cups frozen strawberries (750 mL)
1 cup Da Vinci® Raspberry (250 mL)
 Sugar Free Syrup
1 tbsp orange juice concentrate (15 mL)
2 tsp lemon juice (10 mL)

Yield: 3 cups (750 mL)
$^1/_2$ cup (125 mL) per serving
31.1 calories
0.4 g protein
0.1 g fat
6.5 g carbs

Place strawberries in colander and rinse off any ice crystals. In food processor, with sharp blade, process strawberries on slow speed until coarsely chopped. Add Da Vinci® Raspberry Sugar Free Syrup, orange juice concentrate and lemon juice. Process on medium to high speed until smooth. Serve immediately. Freeze leftovers in closed container and microwave sherbet briefly to serve again later.

Variation: **Da Vinci® Alternative:** Use a berry-flavored sugarless Kool-Aid®, water and a carbohydrate-free sweetener to taste.

CARAMEL TOP HATS

This is a fun dessert which serves many people! Make as many as required.

Sour Cream Mini Pound Cake,
 Page 44, *Splendid Low-Carb*
 Desserts
$^1/_4$ cup Vanilla Ice Cream, (50 mL)
 page 31, *Splendid Low-Carb Desserts*
1 tbsp Caramel Sauce, page 96 (15 mL)

Yield: 1 serving
1 serving
257.4 calories
9.9 g protein
21.4 g fat
7.4 g carbs

Place one slice Sour Cream Mini Pound Cake, page 44, *Splendid Low-Carb Desserts* on a pretty serving plate, and place Vanilla Ice Cream, page 31, *Splendid Low-Carb Desserts* on top. Drizzle Caramel Sauce, page 96 over ice cream.

STRAWBERRY-APPLE ALMOND CRISP

*Delicious with Crème Fraiche, page 99 or Vanilla Ice Cream, page 31 in
Splendid Low-Carb Desserts. Easy!*

3 cups frozen strawberries, (750 mL)
  unsweetened
1 apple, peeled, cored and chopped
$^1/_2$ cup SPLENDA® Granular (125 mL)
$^1/_2$ cup water (125 mL)
1 tbsp lemon juice (15 mL)
1 tsp ThickenThin not/Starch®, (5 mL)
  OR Thickening Agent, page 62
$^2/_3$ cup "Sugared" Almonds, page 98 (150 mL)

Yield: 8 servings
1 serving
120.0 calories
2.9 g protein
7.6 g fat
9.4 g carbs

In medium saucepan, combine strawberries, apple, SPLENDA® Granular, water,
lemon juice and ThickenThin not/Starch or Thickening Agent, page 62. Bring to
boil and cook until apple is tender, stirring occasionally. Pour into shallow 2-
quart (2 L) casserole dish. Allow to cool slightly. Sprinkle with "Sugared"
Almonds, page 98. Serve warm with one of the above suggestions.

LEMON CURD CREAM

*This sweet-tart cream is wonderful served over sliced, fresh strawberries. It
would make a great topping for a lemon pie or a fruit pie or a lemon cheesecake.
Stir into plain yogurt to taste – fabulous!*

3 large egg yolks
6 tbsp SPLENDA® Granular (90 mL)
$^1/_4$ cup lemon juice, (50 mL)
  freshly squeezed (1-2 lemons)
1 tbsp grated lemon peel (15 mL)
4 tbsp unsalted butter (60 mL)
1 cup whipping cream (250 mL)
1 SPLENDA® packet (optional)

Yield: 6 servings
$^1/_3$ cup (75 mL) per serving
236.7 calories
2.4 g protein
24.1 g fat
3.7 g carbs

In double boiler, combine egg yolks, SPLENDA® Granular, lemon juice and
lemon peel. Cook, while stirring, until mixture is fairly thick. Remove from heat
and whisk in butter, one tablespoon (15 mL) at a time, until smooth.

In food processor with whipping assembly, whip cream and SPLENDA®, if
using, until very stiff. Fold into lemon curd. Chill.

STRAWBERRY RHUBARB COBBLER

Cobbler is actually by nature a very carby dessert. In my first diabetic cookbook, Splendid Desserts, a recipe for Summer Fruit Cobbler came in at 32.7 grams carbohydrate per serving out of a yield of 8 servings.

2 cups frozen strawberries, (500 mL) (unsweetened)
2 cups frozen rhubarb (500 mL)
$^2/_3$ cup SPLENDA® Granular (150 mL)
1 tsp lemon juice (5 mL)
2 tbsp water (25 mL)
$^1/_2$ tsp Thickening Agent, page 62 (2 mL)
$2^1/_2$ cups Biskmix™, page 65 (625 mL)
1 tsp baking powder (5 mL)
2 tbsp SPLENDA® Granular (25 mL)
2 tbsp butter, softened (25 mL)
2 tbsp whipping cream (25 mL)

Yield: 8 servings
1 serving
240.0 calories
9.3 g protein
18.8 g fat
8.9 g carbs

In saucepan, combine strawberries, rhubarb, SPLENDA® Granular, lemon juice, water and Thickening Agent, page 62. Bring to boil. Pour hot fruit into shallow 2-quart (2 L) casserole dish.

In medium bowl, combine Biskmix™, page 65, baking powder and SPLENDA® Granular. Rub in butter. Add whipping cream and stir until the mixture forms soft dough that holds together. If it does not hold together, add water by the teaspoonful, stir and repeat until it does. Drop by large spoonfuls onto cobbler filling.

Bake in 400°F (200°C) oven 15 to 17 minutes, or until light golden brown. Serve warm with a dollop Crème Fraiche, page 99 for a really special treat!

Variation: **Strawberry Cobbler:** Use 4 cups (1 L) unsweetened frozen strawberries, $^1/_2$ cup (125 mL) SPLENDA® Granular, 2 tbsp (25 mL) lemon juice, 1 tbsp (15 mL) water and $^1/_2$ tsp Thickening Agent, page 62. (*9.6 g Carbs*)

Helpful Hints: The batter spreads slightly upon baking. It is tender and gives a wonderful melt-in-the-mouth type of experience – a little different to the usual heavy dough type of cobbler we used to have, however, the ground almonds in the Biskmix™, page 65, complement the fruit perfectly. Very tasty!

PIES, CAKES & CHEESECAKES

STRAWBERRY PIE

Sometimes when strawberries first become available in abundance in the Spring, one buys a ton of them, and one wonders what to do with them, before they spoil. This is an easy recipe that will please children especially.

New Single Piecrust, page 80, baked
Filling:
4 cups strawberries, sliced (1 L)
$1^1/_3$ cups water (325 mL)
$1^1/_4$ cups SPLENDA® Granular (300 mL)
$1^1/_2$ tsp Thickening Agent, page 62 (7 mL)
1 envelope sugarless Strawberry, OR
  Wild berry Kool-Aid®
1 envelope unflavored gelatin
2 tbsp water (25 mL)

Yield: 10 servings
1 serving
134.7 calories
7.9 g protein
7.6 g fat
8.0 g carbs

New Single Piecrust: Prepare as directed on page 80. Bake piecrust.

Layer strawberries in baked piecrust, page 80. In medium saucepan, combine $1^1/_3$ cups (325 mL) water, SPLENDA® Granular and Thickening Agent, page 62. Bring to boil. Strain through a sieve, using a spoon to push through sauce and remove from underside of sieve. Stir in Kool-Aid. In cereal bowl, sprinkle gelatin over 2 tbsp (25 mL) water; microwave on high power 45 seconds. Stir into sauce. Let sauce cool slightly and pour over strawberries. Chill thoroughly several hours, or preferably overnight. Serve with Crème Fraiche, page 99, if desired.

~~Bits & Bites~~
For chocolate recipes, combining SPLENDA® Granular and a small amount of erythritol or maltitol (like in a 4:1 ratio) will produce a sweeter result.

NEW SINGLE PIECRUST

This crust is from Splendid Low-Carb Desserts. See below for a variation.

1 $^1/_8$ cups Low-Carb Bake Mix, (275 mL)
  page 64
3 oz cream cheese, softened (90 g)
2 tbsp vital wheat gluten (25 mL)
1 tbsp butter, softened (15 mL)
$^1/_4$ tsp baking soda (1 mL)
$^1/_8$ tsp salt (0.5 mL)

Yield: 10 servings	
1 serving	
99.8 calories	
6.9 g protein	
7.3 g fat	
1.7 g carbs	

In food processor or in bowl with electric mixer, process Low-Carb Bake Mix, page 64, cream cheese, vital wheat gluten, butter, baking soda and salt until mixed. Form a ball with dough using your hands. Chill dough about 1 hour.

Roll dough out between two sheets of wax paper to fit shallow 9-inch (23 cm) glass pie dish with a flat border (do not roll out too thin). Remove top sheet of wax paper. Pick up sheet with dough and invert over pie dish. Use flat dinner knife to carefully ease dough off wax paper. Use small rolling pin or small cylindrical object in pie dish, if necessary, to further roll dough. Patch dough where required.

Press dough onto border, cut to size and patch where necessary. Make an attractive edging by pressing dough with tines of fork and leaving spaces in between. Bake in 350°F (180°C) oven 10 minutes, or until golden brown. This crust browns extremely quickly, so if baking again with filling, it's best to bake only 5 minutes before adding filling and baking. Cover filled pie lightly with foil from beginning of baking to end, otherwise crust becomes too dark. It will still be edible, but it's best to aim for a golden brown color.

Helpful Hints: If using a deep 9-inch (23 cm) pie dish for more substantial fillings, press dough up sides only (straight edge). Push down slightly from edge onto dough with thumbs and this will make a slightly thicker border for the crust. It is possible to skip chilling the dough, however, it is easier to handle when chilled.

~~Bits & Bites~~

The SPLENDA® packets are sweeter than SPLENDA® Granular and one can sometimes get away with 8 packets (8 g carbs) instead of 24 packets (24 g carbs), especially in confections.

APPLE-PEACH LATTICE PIE

This is the crème de la crème of my pie recipes in that it has a fabulous, very substantial double crust with a fruit filling, with the servings still less than 10 grams of carbohydrate! However, do not use a lattice pie crust cutter.

Lattice Piecrust:
$^1/_2$ cup butter, 4 oz {113 g} (125 mL)
$2^1/_3$ cups Low-Carb Bake Mix, (575 mL)
  page 64
2 tbsp vital wheat gluten (25 mL)
$^1/_4$ tsp salt (1 mL)
$^1/_4$ tsp baking powder (1 mL)
$^1/_4$ cup regular cream cheese (50 mL)
2 tbsp ice cold water (25 mL)

Apple-Peach Filling:
4 peaches, peeled, pitted and thinly sliced
$1^1/_2$ apples, peeled, pitted and thinly sliced
1 tbsp lemon juice, optional (15 mL)
8 SPLENDA® packets
$^3/_4$ tsp Thickening Agent, page 62 (3 mL)
$^1/_2$ tsp cinnamon (2 mL)
$^1/_8$ tsp nutmeg (0.5 mL)
1 tbsp butter (15 mL)

Yield: 10/12 servings
1 serving
253.4/211.1 calories
12.2/10.2 g protein
18.5/15.4 g fat
9.7/8.1 g carbs

Lattice Piecrust: Cut butter into cubes; place in plastic wrap and in freezer for half an hour. In food processor, with S-blade, combine Low-Carb Bake Mix, page 64, vital wheat gluten, salt, baking powder and cream cheese; process briefly until mixture resembles coarse meal. Add frozen butter cubes and pulse until butter is no larger than size of a pea. Add ice cold water; process. Form a ball by kneading lightly and then divide into a ratio of $^2/_3 : ^1/_3$. Wrap each ball in plastic wrap and refrigerate 45 minutes. Roll larger ball out between 2 pieces of wax paper to fit 9-inch (23 cm) pie dish with slight overhang. Invert over pie dish and patch where necessary. Pinch to form attractive edge. Refrigerate. Prepare filling. Roll out remaining dough and cut into larger than $^1/_2$-inch (1.3 cm) wide strips. Make a square, by placing 4 overlapping strips around filled pie. Now alternate strips going one way and the other over fruit, leaving spaces. Support strips on flat spatula or cardboard and lay down. Dot with butter between strips.

Apple-Peach Filling: In large bowl, toss peaches and apples with lemon juice (if using). Layer fruit in prepared pie crust. In small bowl, combine SPLENDA®, Thickening Agent, page 62, cinnamon and nutmeg. Sprinkle between fruit layers. Bake prepared pie in 375°F (190°C) oven 20 minutes. Cover with foil. Bake 10 minutes or until fruit is tender. Serve with Crème Fraiche, page 99.

81

CHERRY CHEESE PIE

This fabulous pie is perhaps something one might find in a German or Austrian bakery. Use fresh cherries, pitted, and cut in half, during cherry season.

New Single Piecrust, page 80
  unbaked
Filling:
1 cup fresh cherries, pitted, OR (250 mL)
  canned sweet cherries*
1 1/2 cups cottage cheese (375 mL)
5 oz regular cream cheese (150 g)
2/3 cup SPLENDA® Granular (150 mL)
1 tbsp vital wheat gluten (15 mL)
1 egg
Topping:
1 cup Crème Fraiche, page 99 (250 mL)

Yield: 10 servings
1 serving
242.8 calories
14.4 g protein
17.0 g fat
8.3 g carbs

New Single Piecrust: Prepare single piecrust as directed on page 80 in 9-inch (23 cm) glass pie dish. Make an attractive border out of the dough. Do not bake. Spread pitted coarsely chopped cherries over piecrust.

Filling: In food processor with sharp blade, blender or in bowl with electric mixer, process cottage cheese until smooth. Add cream cheese, SPLENDA® Granular and vital wheat gluten; process. Add egg; process just until smooth. Pour over cherries.

Bake in 350°F (180°C) oven 25 minutes, or until pie is set. Chill. Garnish chilled pie with Crème Fraiche, page 99. Sprinkle with a little grated unsweetened chocolate or garnish with chocolate curls, page 78, *More Splendid Low-Carbing* and a few fresh cherries, if desired.

Helpful Hints: *Canned sweet cherries usually come in a light sugar solution. Drain syrup off. Place cherries in colander and rinse under running water.

Variation: Peach Cheese Pie: Substitute canned, unsweetened sliced peaches for the cherries. (***7.2 g Carbs***).

~~Bits & Bites~~
Although some recipes call for Da Vinci® Sugar Free Syrups, I usually endeavor to provide an alternative.

BUMBLE BERRY TART

Raspberries and blueberries make an eye-catching presentation.

New Single Piecrust, page 80
Filling:
$^2/_3$ cup SPLENDA® Granular (150 mL)
2 tbsp vital wheat gluten (25 mL)
1 tbsp whole wheat pastry flour (15 mL)
$^1/_4$ tsp cinnamon (1 mL)
$^1/_8$ tsp salt (0.5 mL)
2 cups fresh raspberries (500 mL)
2 cups fresh blueberries (500 mL)
1 tbsp butter (15 mL)
Topping (optional):
Crème Fraiche, page 99

Yield: 10 servings
1 serving
136.2 calories
8.5 g protein
7.6 g fat
7.4 g carbs

New Single Piecrust: Prepare as directed on page 80 in shallow 9-inch (23 cm) glass pie dish, but do not bake.

Filling: In small bowl, combine SPLENDA® Granular, vital wheat gluten, whole wheat pastry flour, cinnamon and salt. Sprinkle half this mixture over pastry shell. Top with half the berries, the rest of the dry ingredient mixture and remaining berries. Bake in 400°F (200°C) oven on lowest rack. Check pie after 20 minutes. Cover with foil tent and bake another 5 to 10 minutes, if necessary. Refrigerate. Serve chilled pie with Crème Fraiche, page 99 for a really super treat. Garnish pie with a few extra raspberries, if desired.

BISKMIX™ BUTTERMILK PIE

Delicious, delicate crust forms on top of this easy, sweet pie. My DH's favorite.

$1^1/_2$ cups SPLENDA® Granular (375 mL)
1 cup buttermilk (250 mL)
$^2/_3$ cup Biskmix™, page 65 (150 mL)
$^1/_2$ cup butter, melted (125 mL)
3 eggs, fork beaten
1 tsp vanilla extract (5 mL)

Yield: 10 servings
1 serving
167.0 calories
4.7 g protein
14.1 g fat
4.7 g carbs

In medium bowl, combine SPLENDA® Granular, buttermilk, Biskmix™, page 65, butter, eggs and vanilla extract. Pour into greased 9-inch (23 cm) glass baking dish. Bake in 350°F (180°C) oven 40 minutes, or until set.

BISKMIX™ APPLE CRUMBLE PIE

My family loved this pie – tastes like the real thing! I adapted a recipe that my good friend, Linda Parsons, who is from Georgia, gave me at the end of writing this cookbook. I had one extra page left after completing the index and made this pie a couple of days before the book went to the printers. Enjoy!

3 cups sliced peeled apples (750 mL)
1$\frac{1}{2}$ tsp ground cinnamon (7 mL)
$\frac{2}{3}$ cup Biskmix™, page 65 (150 mL)
$\frac{1}{2}$ cup SPLENDA® Granular (125 mL)
$\frac{1}{4}$ cup water (50 mL)
3 tbsp whipping cream (45 mL)
1 tbsp butter, softened (15 mL)
2 eggs, fork beaten
Crumble Topping:
$\frac{2}{3}$ cup Biskmix™, page 65 (150 mL)
$\frac{1}{4}$ cup chopped nuts (50 mL)
  (I used pecans and cashews)
$\frac{1}{4}$ cup SPLENDA® Granular (50 mL)
2 tbsp cold butter (25 mL)

Yield: 10 servings
1 serving
173.1 calories
5.8 g protein
13.0 g fat
8.6 g carbs

In medium bowl, combine apples and cinnamon. In small bowl, combine Biskmix™, page 65, SPLENDA® Granular, water, whipping cream, butter and eggs. Spray 9-inch (23 cm) glass pie dish with nonstick cooking spray. Arrange apples in pie dish. Pour custard mixture over apple pie. Sprinkle with Crumble Topping. Bake in 325°F (160°C) oven 40 to 45 minutes, or until knife inserted in center comes out clean and crumble is nicely browned. Serve warm with Crème Fraiche, page 99 or Vanilla Ice Cream, page 31 in *Splendid Low-Carb Desserts.*

Crumble Topping: In small bowl, combine Biskmix™, page 65, chopped nuts and SPLENDA® Granular. Rub in cold butter with fingers.

~~*Bits & Bites*~~
*Eating a low sodium diet makes for stable weight practically every day.
Nowadays there are so many wonderful spices that help make food taste good.*

BISKMIX™ COCONUT CUSTARD PIE

Very tasty pie forms its own crust on top.

1 cup whipping cream (250 mL)
1 cup water (250 mL)
1 cup finely desiccated coconut, (250 mL)
 (unsweetened)
1 cup SPLENDA® Granular (250 mL)
$^2/_3$ cup Biskmik, page 65 (150 mL)
$^1/_4$ cup butter, melted (50 mL)
3 eggs, well beaten with fork
$1^1/_2$ tsp vanilla extract (7 mL)

Yield: 10 servings
1 serving
256.7 calories
4.9 g protein
23.7.2 g fat
4.4 g carbs

In large bowl, combine whipping cream, water, coconut, SPLENDA® Granular, Biskmix™, page 65, butter, eggs and vanilla extract. Pour into 9-inch (23 cm) glass pie dish sprayed with nonstick cooking spray. Bake in 350°F (180°C) oven 50 minutes or until set and turning light brown. Serve warm or cold.

PEACH COFFEE CAKE

Lovely, moist coffee cake using fresh peaches.

$^1/_2$ cup butter, softened (125 mL)
1 egg
$1^1/_2$ cups SPLENDA® Granular (375 mL)
1 tsp molasses, optional (5 mL)
$2^1/_4$ cups Low-Carb Bake Mix, (550 mL)
 page 64
1 tsp baking soda (5 mL)
$^3/_4$ cup buttermilk (175 mL)
3 peaches, peeled and diced
$^1/_3$ cup "Sugared Almonds", page 98 (75 mL)

Yield: 15 servings
1 serving
177.6 calories
8.3 g protein
13.3 g fat
6.1 g carbs

In food processor, process butter and egg. Add SPLENDA® Granular and molasses (if using); process. Add Low-Carb Bake Mix, page 64 and baking soda alternately with buttermilk, processing until smooth after each addition. Gently fold in peaches. Pour batter into lightly greased 9 x 13-inch (23 x 33 cm) glass baking dish and spread evenly. Sprinkle with "Sugared Almonds", page 98.

Bake in 350°F (180°C) oven 25 to 30 minutes, or until knife inserted in cake comes out clean. Serve with a dollop Crème Fraiche, page 99.

85

PUMPKIN CAKE ROLL

A beautiful cake, suitable for any occasion.

3 eggs
1 cup SPLENDA® Granular (250 mL)
$^2/_3$ cup canned pumpkin (150 mL)
1 cup Low-Carb Bake Mix, (250 mL)
 page 64
1$^1/_2$ tsp pumpkin pie spice, page 58 (7 mL)
1 tsp baking powder (5 mL)
$^1/_4$ tsp salt (1 mL)
1 tbsp Confectioner's Sugar Substitute, (15 mL)
 page 97

Yield: 12 servings
1 slice per serving
175.5 calories
7.4 g protein
13.8 g fat
5.7 g carbs

Filling:
8 oz regular cream cheese, softened (250 g)
$^1/_2$ cup SPLENDA® Granular (125 mL)
$^1/_4$ cup unsalted butter, softened (50 mL)
1 tbsp Da Vinci® Sugar Free (15 mL)
 French Vanilla Syrup, OR
 $^1/_2$ tsp (2 mL) vanilla extract and water

Line 15 x 10-inch (38 x 25 cm) jelly roll pan with wax paper. Spray liberally with nonstick cooking spray and sprinkle with a tiny amount of bake mix.

In food processor, or in bowl with electric mixer, process eggs 4 minutes on medium high speed. While processing, gradually add SPLENDA® Granular. Add pumpkin; process on lower speed.

In medium bowl, combine Low-Carb Bake Mix, page 64, pumpkin pie spice, page 58, baking powder and salt. Make a well in center and add pumpkin mixture. Combine well. Pour over prepared pan and spread out evenly. Bake in 375°F (190°C) oven 15 minutes. Invert cake onto clean tea towel. Carefully remove wax paper. Gently roll up cake from one short side (it will probably crack, but just keep going slowly) together with towel. Set aside to cool completely. Gently unroll and spread with cream cheese filling, sealing crack. Again roll up cake from short side. Sprinkle with Confectioner's Sugar Substitute, page 97.

Filling: In food processor with S-blade, in blender, or in bowl with electric mixer, process cream cheese, SPLENDA® Granular, butter and Da Vinci® Sugar Free French Vanilla Syrup or vanilla extract and water.

DELUXE CARROT CAKE

When I first tasted my Aunt Marie Richardson's carrot cake, I knew I had to make a low-carb version. Enjoy!

4 eggs
$2^1/_4$ cups Low-Carb Bake Mix, (550 mL)
  page 64
$1^1/_2$ cups SPLENDA® Granular (375 mL)
2 tsp baking powder (10 mL)
$1^1/_2$ tsp baking soda (7 mL)
1 tsp cinnamon (5 mL)
$^1/_2$ tsp salt (2 mL)
$^3/_4$ cup olive oil (175 mL)
1 cup grated zucchini (250 mL)
1 cup grated carrot (250 mL)
$^1/_2$ cup drained, crushed pineapple (125 mL)
$^1/_4$ cup chopped pecans (50 mL)

Cream Cheese Frosting:
6 oz light cream cheese (180 g)
4 SPLENDA® packets
3 tbsp butter, softened (45 mL)
2 tbsp whipping cream (25 mL)
1 tsp vanilla extract (5 mL)

Yield: 18 servings
1 serving
228.2 calories
7.9 g protein
19.5 g fat
5.4 g carbs

Line a Bundt pan with wax paper and spray liberally with nonstick cooking spray. In food processor with S-blade or in bowl with electric mixer, process eggs. In medium bowl, combine Low-Carb Bake Mix, page 64, SPLENDA® Granular, baking powder, baking soda, cinnamon and salt. Add half dry ingredients and olive oil to eggs; process. Repeat. The batter will be very thick. In medium bowl, combine zucchini, carrot, pineapple and pecans. Stir into carrot cake batter and pour into prepared pan. Bake in 350°F (180°C) oven 35 to 40 minutes or until a knife inserted in cake comes out clean. Cover with foil and bake another 20 minutes, or until a knife inserted in cake comes out clean. Loosen cooled cake from around funnel with a knife. Invert cake over cake rack. Carefully remove wax paper. Refrigerate frosted Carrot Cake.

Cream Cheese Frosting: In food processor with S-blade, in blender or in bowl with electric mixer, process cream cheese with SPLENDA®, butter, whipping cream and vanilla extract until smooth. Spread over top of cooled cake.

Helpful Hints: I line my Bundt pan with wax paper (make a hole for center funnel), as often low-carb baking will stick to even nonstick pans. Cut bigger folds off. This cake freezes well (if frosted, slice and freeze in sealed container).

KATHY'S SOUR CREAM COFFEE CAKE

Kathy Gallagher, an occupational therapist, has been our friend for many years. She lives in beautiful Victoria, B.C. She says this favorite recipe of hers for coffee cake (which she enjoys for breakfast) originated with her grandmother.

4 oz butter, softened (125 g)
1 cup SPLENDA® Granular (250 mL)
2 eggs
2$\frac{1}{4}$ cups Low-Carb Bake Mix, (550 mL)
  page 64
1 tsp baking powder (5 mL)
1 tsp baking soda (5 mL)
1 cup sour cream (250 mL)

Sweet Cinnamon-nut mixture:
$\frac{1}{2}$ cup chopped pecans, OR (125 mL)
  your choice of nuts
$\frac{1}{3}$ cup SPLENDA® Granular (75 mL)
$\frac{1}{2}$ tsp cinnamon (2 mL)

Cream Cheese Drizzle (optional):
4 oz light cream cheese, softened (125 g)
$\frac{1}{3}$ cup SPLENDA® Granular (75 mL)
2 tbsp unsalted butter, softened (25 mL)
2 tbsp Da Vinci® Sugar Free Vanilla Syrup* (25 mL)
1 tbsp whipping cream (15 mL)

Yield: 16/18 servings
1 serving
183.6/163.2 calories
7.6/6.8 g protein
15.2/13.5 g fat
4.6/4.1 g carbs

In food processor with S-blade or in bowl with electric mixer, cream butter. Add SPLENDA® Granular and eggs; process. In medium bowl, combine Low-Carb Bake Mix, baking powder and baking soda; stir. Add half dry ingredients and sour cream; process. Repeat.

Sweet Cinnamon-nut Mixture: In small bowl, combine chopped pecans, SPLENDA® Granular and cinnamon.

Line 9-inch (23 cm) Bundt pan with wax paper. Spray well, including funnel, with nonstick cooking spray. Arrange in alternating layers of cake batter and nut mixture, ending with the latter. Bake in 350°F (180°C) oven 30 to 40 minutes, or until knife inserted in cake comes out clean. Loosen cooled cake around funnel and invert over wire rack.

Cream Cheese Drizzle (optional): In food processor with S-blade or in blender, process cream cheese, SPLENDA® Granular, butter, Da Vinci® Sugar Free Vanilla Syrup (*or water and $\frac{1}{4}$ tsp (1 mL) vanilla extract) and whipping cream. Drizzle over cooled cake. (**5.4/4.8 g Carbs**)

PUMPKIN CHEESECAKE

This is an unusual way of making pumpkin cheesecake with cooked eggs and not baked. Jonathan loved it so much, that the two cheesecakes made back-to-back were consumed in no time flat.

Ginger Crust:
$^2/_3$ cup Low-Carb Bake Mix, (150 mL) page 64
$^2/_3$ cup ground almonds (150 mL)
$^1/_3$ cup butter, melted (75 mL)
2 SPLENDA® packets
$^1/_2$ tsp ground ginger (2 mL)

Filling:
16 oz regular cream cheese, (500 g) softened
14 oz canned pumpkin (398 mL)
1 cup SPLENDA® Granular (250 mL)
3 eggs
1 tsp cinnamon (5 mL)
$^1/_2$ tsp ground ginger (2 mL)
1 envelope unflavored gelatin, PLUS 1$^1/_2$ tsp (7 mL)
$^1/_2$ cup Da Vinci® Sugar Free Vanilla (125 mL) Syrup
$^1/_2$ cup whipping cream (125 mL)

> **Yield:** 12/16 servings
> 1 serving
> 304.6/228.4 calories
> 10.1/7.6 g protein
> 26.3/19.7 g fat
> **7.1/5.4 g carbs**

Ginger Crust: In medium bowl, combine Low-Carb Bake Mix, page 64, ground almonds, butter, SPLENDA® and ground ginger. Press into 9-inch (23 cm) springform pan. Bake in 350°F (180°C) oven 10 minutes, or until turning brown.

Filling: In food processor with S-blade, in blender or in bowl with electric mixer, process cream cheese until smooth.

In medium, nonstick saucepan, combine pumpkin, SPLENDA® Granular, eggs, cinnamon, ginger and gelatin. Stir over medium heat until very hot. Add to cream cheese; process. Add Da Vinci® Sugar Free Vanilla Syrup and whipping cream; process. Pour over prepared crust. Chill 24 hours before serving.

Variation: Da Vinci® Alternative: Use 1 tsp (5 mL) vanilla extract, water and $^1/_4$ cup (50 mL) SPLENDA® Granular. (*7.6/5.8 g carbs*)

CHOCOLATE ECSTASY CHEESECAKE

Tunnels of gooey chocolate sauce built into a velvety-smooth cheesecake makes for a very sensual experience says Jeanne Lobsinger, who is like a mother to me.

Graham Cracker-like Crust:
$^2/_3$ cup Low-Carb Bake Mix, (150 mL)
  Page 64
$^2/_3$ cup ground almonds (150 mL)
$^1/_3$ cup butter, melted (75 mL)
2 SPLENDA® packets

Filling:
16 oz regular cream cheese, (500 g)
  softened
1 cup SPLENDA® Granular (250 mL)
1 cup whipping cream (250 mL)
$1^1/_2$ envelopes unflavored gelatin (22 mL)
$^1/_4$ cup water (50 mL)

Condensed Milk Chocolate Sauce, page 96

Yield: 16 servings
1 serving
314.0 calories
8.7 g protein
28.7 g fat
6.6 g carbs

Graham Cracker-like Crust: In medium bowl, combine Low-Carb Bake Mix, page 64, ground almonds, butter and SPLENDA®. Press into 9-inch (23 cm) springform pan. Bake in 350°F (180°C) oven 10 minutes, or until turning brown.

Filling: In food processor with S-blade, blender or in bowl with electric mixer, process cream cheese and SPLENDA® Granular until smooth. Add whipping cream gradually while processing. In cereal bowl, combine gelatin and water. Microwave 45 seconds. Add gelatin mixture to cream cheese mixture along with $^3/_4$ cup (175 mL) Condensed Milk Chocolate Sauce, page 96; process.

Pour over prepared crust. Pour remaining sauce over cheesecake in 5 blobs, placed randomly. Use flat, dinner knife to gently swirl between the blobs. Chill.

Condensed Milk Chocolate Sauce: Prepare as directed on page 96.

Variation: Frozen Chocolate Ecstasy Cheesecake: Freeze cheesecake and let thaw at room temperature at least 20 minutes, or until easy to slice, before serving.

Helpful Hint: For a really creamy taste experience, leave cheesecake at room temperature for 30 minutes to 1 hour.

PRALINES 'N CARAMEL CHEESECAKE

Very unusual, flavorful cheesecake with caramel sauce that has a distinct condensed milk-like and caramel taste.

Praline Crust:
$^3/_4$ cup finely chopped pecans (175 mL)
6 SPLENDA® packets
$^1/_8$ tsp cinnamon (0.5 mL)
3 tbsp butter, melted (45 mL)
Filling:
16 oz regular cream cheese, (500 g)
   softened
1 cup SPLENDA® Granular (250 mL)
$1^1/_2$ tsp vanilla extract (7 mL)
1 cup whipping cream (250 mL)
$1^1/_2$ envelopes unflavored gelatin (22 mL)
$^1/_4$ cup water (50 mL)
Caramel Sauce, page 96

> **Yield:** 12/16 servings
> 1 serving
> 385.0/288.8 calories
> 7.9/5.9 g protein
> 36.0/27.0 g fat
> **8.6/6.4 g carbs**

Praline Crust: In medium bowl, combine pecans, SPLENDA®, cinnamon and melted butter. Press into 9-inch (23 cm) springform pan. Bake in 350°F (180°C) oven 5 minutes.

Filling: In food processor with sharp blade, blender or in bowl with electric mixer, process cream cheese, SPLENDA® Granular and vanilla extract until smooth. Add whipping cream gradually while processing. In cereal bowl, combine gelatin and water. Microwave 45 seconds. Add to cream cheese mixture along with $^3/_4$ cup (175 mL) Caramel Sauce, page 96; process.

Pour over prepared crust. Pour remaining sauce over cheesecake in 5 blobs here and there. Use a flat, dinner knife to gently swirl between the blobs. Chill.

Caramel Sauce: Prepare as directed on page 96.

Variation: Frozen Pralines 'N Caramel Cheesecake: Freeze cheesecake and let thaw at room temperature at least 20 minutes, or until easy to slice, before serving. The sauce will obviously be frozen as well and the cheesecake will be firm throughout. It is not icy, but a smooth, frozen treat!

~~Bits & Bites~~
The advantage of using Da Vinci® Sugar Free Syrups is that it helps sweeten desserts, sauces and drinks, for example, with virtually no additional carbs.

BLACK BOTTOM PEANUT BUTTER CHEESECAKE

A smooth, creamy cheesecake. Instead of Da Vinci® Sugar Free Syrup, you can use water, extra sweetener to taste and vanilla extract.

Chocolate Crust:

1$^1/_2$ oz light cream cheese, softened (45 g)
2 tbsp unsalted butter, softened (25 mL)
$^1/_4$ cup cocoa (50 mL)
$^1/_4$ cup SPLENDA® Granular (50 mL)
3 tbsp vital wheat gluten (45 mL)
2 tbsp whipping cream (25 mL)

Yield: 12/16 servings
1 serving
328.2/246.1 calories
11.0/8.3 g protein
28.9/21.7 g fat
6.8/5.1 g carbs

Chocolate Layer:

3 tbsp Dutch cocoa (45 mL)
3 tbsp Da Vinci® Sugar Free (45 mL) Chocolate, Peanut Butter, or Vanilla Syrup
4 SPLENDA® packets
$^1/_2$ cup sugarless chocolate chips, optional (125 mL)

Filling:

24 oz regular cream cheese, softened (750 g)
$^1/_2$ cup peanut butter (125 mL)
12 SPLENDA® packets
1 cup Da Vinci® Sugar Free Peanut Butter, OR Vanilla Syrup (250 mL)
$^1/_4$ cup whipping cream (50 mL)
$^1/_4$ cup Da Vinci® Sugar Free Peanut Butter, OR Vanilla Syrup (50 mL)
1 envelope unflavored gelatin
1 tbsp grated unsweetened chocolate (15 mL)

Chocolate Crust: In food processor, process cream cheese and butter until smooth. Add cocoa, SPLENDA® Granular, vital wheat gluten and whipping cream; process. Spread in 9-inch (23 cm) springform pan. Cover with plastic wrap and press crust out evenly. Bake in 350°F (180°C) oven 5 minutes.

Chocolate Layer: In small bowl, whisk together Dutch cocoa, Da Vinci® Sugar Free Peanut Butter, Chocolate or Vanilla Syrup (see alternatives below title) and SPLENDA®. Spread over chocolate crust; sprinkle with chocolate chips, if using.

Filling: In food processor with S-blade, in blender, or in bowl with electric mixer, process cream cheese, peanut butter and SPLENDA® until smooth. Gradually, while processing, add 1 cup (250 mL) Da Vinci® Sugar Free Peanut Butter or Vanilla Syrup and whipping cream. In bowl, pour $^1/_4$ cup (50 mL) Da Vinci® Sugar Free Syrup and stir in gelatin. Microwave 45 seconds. Add to cheesecake batter and process until combined. Pour over prepared crust. Sprinkle with grated chocolate. Chill.

MOCHA SOUR CREAM CHEESECAKE

A large, solid cheesecake that will appeal more to adult tastes.

Graham Cracker-like Crust:
$^2/_3$ cup Low-Carb Bake Mix, (150 mL)
  page 64
$^2/_3$ cup ground almonds (150 mL)
$^1/_3$ cup butter, melted (75 mL)
2 SPLENDA® packets

Filling:
32 oz regular cream cheese, (1 kg)
  softened
1 cup SPLENDA® Granular (250 mL)
24 SPLENDA® packets
4 eggs
1 cup sour cream (250 mL)
$^1/_2$ cup Da Vinci® Sugar Free Kahlua Syrup (125 mL)
$^1/_4$ cup whipping cream (50 mL)
2 oz unsweetened chocolate, melted (60 g)

Optional Garnish:
1 cup Crème Fraiche, page 99 (250 mL)

Yield: 16 servings
1 serving
349.8 calories
10.8 g protein
31.4 g fat
7.1 g carbs

Graham Cracker-like Crust: In medium bowl, combine Low-Carb Bake Mix, page 64, ground almonds, butter and SPLENDA®. Press into 9-inch (23 cm) springform pan. Bake in 350°F (180°C) oven 10 minutes, or until turning brown.

Filling: In food processor, process cream cheese until very smooth. Add SPLENDA® Granular, SPLENDA® and add eggs, one at a time, while processing. Add sour cream, Da Vinci® Sugar Free Kahlua Syrup and whipping cream; process. Add melted chocolate; process. Pour filling over prepared crust and bake in 325°F (160°C) oven 1 hour. Switch oven off and allow cheesecake to remain inside until it reaches room temperature. When cool, cover with plastic wrap and chill. Before serving, garnish with Crème Fraiche, page 99, if desired.

Variation: Da Vinci® Alternative: Combine $^1/_2$ cup (125 mL) water, 2 SPLENDA® packets and 2 tsp (10 mL) instant coffee granules.

~~Bits & Bites~~

If I was to buy only one Da Vinci® Sugar Free Syrup, it would be the vanilla flavor, as it can often be substituted in recipes calling for another flavor. Just use an extract or something else to enhance the flavor in the direction required.

CONFECTIONS & FROSTINGS

PEANUT BUTTER CUPS

*There is a taste explosion when one bites into one of these substantial treats!
They look really attractive too.*

1.5 oz cocoa butter (45 g)
1 oz unsweetened chocolate (30 g)
$^1/_4$ cup peanut butter, softened (50 mL)
$^1/_4$ cup butter, melted (50 mL)
2 tbsp whole, OR skim milk (25 mL)
  powder
1 tbsp whipping cream (15 ml)
10 SPLENDA® packets

Yield: 10 servings
1 serving
139.8 calories
2.2 g protein
13.7 g fat
3.0 g carbs

In cereal bowl, microwave cocoa butter and chocolate on high power 2 minutes. Stir cocoa butter until it melts. If necessary, nuke in microwave oven 30 to 60 seconds more, however be careful of overheating chocolate, or it could seize and taste really bitter as a result. In another cereal bowl, soften peanut butter 30 seconds on high power in microwave oven. Stir peanut butter, butter, whole or skim milk powder, whipping cream and SPLENDA® into chocolate mixture. Pour into small milk jug.

Carefully pour and half fill 10 medium paper baking cups placed on two dinner plates or a cookie sheet. Keep them in the freezer. Remove paper to serve.

Variation: **Almond Butter Cups:** Use almond butter instead of peanut butter. (*3.1 g Carbs*).

Helpful Hints: I used finely ground whole milk powder. Carnation® skim milk powder will be fine, but really coarse skim milk powder may have to be blended finely first for best results.

~~Bits & Bites~~
Yogurt is very beneficial for weight loss. 1 cup (250 mL) has only 4 g carbs, since the live bacteria have changed the lactose into lactic acid, and this is not taken into account in the nutritional analysis. The Go Diet Authors made me aware of this fact, when they brought to light recent laboratory research.

MELTING MOMENTS CHOCOLATE

As the title suggests, this milk chocolate melts in your mouth. It is quite sweet.

1 oz unsweetened chocolate (30 g)
1 oz cocoa butter (30 g)
$^1/_4$ cup unsalted butter (50 mL)
$^1/_4$ cup Crème Fraiche, page 99 (50 mL)
24 SPLENDA® packets
$^1/_4$ cup finely ground skim milk (50 mL)
  powder

> **Yield:** 18 (6 x 3) pieces
> 1 thick piece
> 59.6 calories
> 0.6 g protein
> 5.6 g fat
> **2.3 g carbs**

In cereal bowl, microwave chocolate and cocoa butter on high power 2 minutes. In medium bowl, melt butter, approximately 50 seconds, in microwave oven. Whisk Crème Fraiche, page 99 into butter. Add SPLENDA® and whisk to combine. Add to chocolate and whisk to combine. Whisk in skim milk powder. Pour into $5^3/_4$ x $3^1/_4$ x $2^1/_4$ inch (15 x 8 x 6 cm) mini loaf pan. Freeze or freeze and refrigerate for a creamy, fairly solid fudge.

Variation: **Dark Chocolate Melting Moments:** Use 2 oz (60 g) unsweetened baking chocolate. Omit cocoa butter. (*2.4 g Carbs*)

BUTTERSCOTCH WHITE CHOCOLATE

Upon tasting it, Jonathan said, "This tastes like white chocolate with a butterscotch flavor." That's basically what this is. It is quite sweet.

4 oz cocoa butter (120 g)
$^1/_2$ cup whipping cream (125 mL)
1 package Jello® Diet Pudding (40 g)
  (Butterscotch flavor)
32 SPLENDA® packets
$^1/_2$ cup sour cream (125 mL)
$^1/_4$ cup vanilla whey protein (50 mL)
$^1/_3$ cup "Sugared" Almonds, (75 mL)
  Page 98, (optional)

> **Yield:** 36 large pieces
> 1 piece
> 45.9 calories
> 0.6 g protein
> 4.1 g fat
> **1.8 g carbs**

In double boiler, combine cocoa butter and whipping cream. Melt cocoa butter over medium heat. Remove from heat Add Jello® Diet Pudding (butterscotch flavor) and SPLENDA® to cocoa butter-cream mixture, along with sour cream. Combine and whisk in vanilla whey protein. Spread evenly in an 8-inch (20 cm) glass baking dish. Sprinkle with "Sugared Almonds," page 98, if using. Freeze.

CONDENSED MILK CHOCOLATE SAUCE
Decadent!

$^1/_2$ cup whipping cream (125 mL)
$^1/_3$ cup butter, melted (75 mL)
$^1/_3$ cup Da Vinci® Sugar Free (75 mL)
 French Vanilla or Vanilla Syrup
1 cup SPLENDA® Granular (250 mL)
$^1/_3$ cup vanilla whey protein (75 mL)
$^1/_3$ cup skim milk powder, OR (75 mL)
 whole milk powder
$^1/_8$ tsp Thickening Agent, page 62 (0.5 mL)
1 oz unsweetened chocolate, melted (30 g)

Yield: $1^2/_3$ cups (400 mL)
1 tbsp (15 mL) per serving
51.1 calories
1.4 g protein
4.5 g fat
1.7 g carbs

In blender, combine whipping cream, butter, Da Vinci® Sugar Free French Vanilla or Vanilla Syrup, SPLENDA® Granular, vanilla whey protein, skim or whole milk powder and Thickening Agent, page 62. Blend until smooth. Add melted chocolate; blend. Serve immediately or refrigerate and use later.

Variations: **Condensed Milk Chocolate Frosting:** Use $^1/_3$ cup (75 mL) whipping cream and 2 tbsp (25 mL) Da Vinci® Sugar Free Vanilla Syrup. *Yield:* 1 cup (250 mL). 12/16/36 servings: 100.5/75.4/33.5 calories, 2.9/2.2/1.0g protein, 8.6/6.4/2.9g fat, 3.7/2.8/1.3g carbs.

Caramel Sauce/Frosting: Substitute Da Vinci® Sugar Free Caramel Syrup in main recipe and use cocoa butter instead of chocolate. Follow instructions for variation above for frosting as opposed to the sauce in the main recipe.

Any-Flavor Sauce: Cocoa butter and Da Vinci® Sugar Free Syrup flavor of choice or chocolate and Da Vinci® Sugar Free Syrup flavor of choice.

Da Vinci® Alternative: Use water, appropriate flavored extract and 1 or 2 SPLENDA® packets.

Helpful Hints: This sauce is thick and becomes a little thicker upon chilling. Xanthan gum or guar gum may be used instead of Thickening Agent, page 62.

~~Bits & Bites~~
Anytime you make a treat and feel you cannot control your portions, quickly freeze the remainder and bring it out only when you feel your will power is stronger or you have others around to help you finish it.

CONFECTIONER'S SUGAR SUBSTITUTE

I usually include in each new book 4 or 5 recipes from previous cookbooks, which will be required, for convenience. This is particularly important for those folks who could only afford to buy one of my cookbooks.

2$^1/_4$ cups SPLENDA® Granular (550 mL)
1$^1/_3$ cups whole milk powder* (325 mL)
 (finely ground)
$^2/_3$ cup vanilla whey protein (150 mL)

Yield: 4 cups (1 L)
1 tbsp (15 mL) per serving
19.7 calories
1.4 g protein
0.7 g fat
1.9 g carbs

In large bowl, combine SPLENDA® Granular, whole milk powder and vanilla whey protein.

Helpful Hint: *Skim milk powder may be used instead, however, blend finely in blender in batches first, if is the coarse kind, before combining with remaining ingredients.

DARK CHOCOLATE ALMOND BARK

Very dark, semi-sweet chocolate.

3 egg yolks
$^1/_4$ cup whipping cream (50 mL)
32 SPLENDA® packets
$^1/_4$ cup butter (50 mL)
4 oz unsweetened chocolate, (120 g)
 melted
$^1/_4$ cup whipping cream (50 mL)
$^1/_4$ cup skim, OR whole milk (50 mL)
 powder (finely ground)
$^1/_2$ cup coarsely chopped raw almonds (125 mL)

Yield: 36 pieces
1 piece
63.8 calories
1.3 g protein
5.9 g fat
1.9 g carbs

In double boiler, over medium heat, whisk egg yolks, whipping cream and SPLENDA® until thickened. Whisk in butter until melted. Stir in melted chocolate until smooth. Stir in whipping cream and skim or whole milk powder. Stir in almonds. Spread evenly in 8-inch (20 cm) glass baking dish and spread out evenly. Freeze.

"SUGARED" ALMONDS

Good as a topping for salads or chocolate or other desserts. The indicated serving size is usually sufficient.

2 tsp butter (10 mL)
1 cup sliced almonds (250 mL)
$^{1}/_{4}$ cup SPLENDA® Granular (50 mL)
$^{1}/_{4}$ tsp cinnamon, optional (1 mL)

> **Yield:** 3 servings
> $^{1}/_{3}$ cup (75 mL) per serving
> 329.7 calories
> 10.5 g protein
> 29.4 g fat
> **5.8 g carbs**

In large frying pan, melt butter. Add almonds and stir-fry until turning golden brown. Remove from heat and stir in SPLENDA® Granular and cinnamon, if using.

"SUGARED" ALMOND CHOCOLATE

Dutch cocoa is used to make this easy chocolate.

6 tbsp unsalted butter (90 mL)
6 tbsp whipping cream (90 mL)
6 tbsp Dutch cocoa (90 mL)
3 tbsp almond butter (45 mL)
2 tbsp skim milk powder (25 mL)
20 SPLENDA® packets
1 tsp vanilla extract (5 mL)
$^{1}/_{3}$ cup "Sugared" Almonds, (75 mL)
  page 98

> **Yield:** 36 pieces
> 1 serving
> 47.7 calories
> 0.8 g protein
> 4.4 g fat
> **1.3 g carbs**

In double boiler, combine butter, whipping cream, Dutch cocoa, almond butter, skim milk powder and SPLENDA®. When butter melts, whisk until smooth and stir in vanilla extract.

Pour into 8-inch (20 cm) glass baking dish. Spread evenly. Sprinkle with "Sugared" Almonds, page 98. Press into chocolate slightly. Freeze in freezer above refrigerator.

CRÈME FRAICHE

Lovely sweetened whipped topping for serving with desserts or for garnishing desserts. It holds up better than plain whipped cream and tastes better.

1 cup whipping cream (250 mL)
$^1/_2$ cup SPLENDA® Granular (125 mL)
$^1/_4$ tsp Thickening Agent, page 62 (1 mL)
 (optional)
$^2/_3$ cup regular sour cream, OR (150 mL)
 nonfat sour cream
$^1/_2$ tsp vanilla extract (2 mL)

Yield: $2^1/_8$ cups (525 mL)
2 tbsp (25 mL) per serving
56.2 calories
0.5 g protein
5.4 g fat
1.5 g carbs

In food processor, on low speed, process whipping cream with SPLENDA® Granular. While processing, sprinkle in Thickening Agent, page 62, if using, through feed tube. Process until thick. Add sour cream and vanilla extract; process on medium high speed just until combined. It will keep at least one week or longer in the refrigerator.

Variation: **Lower Carb Alternative:** Omit SPLENDA® Granular. Use $^1/_2$ tsp (2 mL) to $^3/_4$ tsp (3 mL) Thickening Agent, page 62. Use $^1/_4$ cup (50 mL) Da Vinci® Sugar Free Syrup such as Vanilla or French Vanilla instead of SPLENDA® Granular. Process whipping cream and Thickening Agent, page 62, until thick. Add syrup along with sour cream; process.
2 tbsp (25 mL) per serving: (53.6 calories, 0.5 g protein, 5.4 g fat, *0.8 g carbs*)

Helpful Hints: Thickening Agent, page 62, makes Crème Fraiche firmer and easier to garnish desserts using a pastry bag. Double Thickening agent, page 62, for thicker Crème Fraiche.

This topping is wonderful on fresh fruit salad or fresh strawberries. In my opinion, it tastes better than sweetened whipped cream. Recipe may easily be doubled or halved.

Half this recipe will suffice as a topping for a cheesecake.
Yield: 12 servings. 1 serving: (42.0 calories, 0.4 g protein, 4.1 g fat, *1.1 g carbs*)

~~Bits & Bites~~
A high sodium diet is never a good idea in my opinion. Besides the distressing water weight factor (even one's jeans feel tighter), it can lead to hypertension.

COOKIES & SQUARES

FAVORITE CHOCOLATE CHIP COOKIES

These crunchy cookies will totally surprise your friends who are not into low-carbing! There are chocolate chips available that are sweetened with sucralose.

$1^1/_2$ cups SPLENDA® Granular (375 mL)
1 cup butter, softened (250 mL)
1 egg
1 tsp molasses (5 mL)
$2^1/_2$ cups Low-Carb Bake Mix, (625 mL)
  Page 64
1 tsp baking soda (5 mL)
$^1/_2$ tsp salt* (2 mL)
2 cups sugar free chocolate chips** (500 mL)
1 cup chopped pecans, OR (250 mL)
  walnuts, OR mixed nuts

Yield: 52 cookies
1 cookie per serving
103.7 calories
2.7 g protein
8.2 g fat
1.9 g carbs

In food processor or in bowl with electric mixer, combine SPLENDA® Granular, butter, egg and molasses; process. In medium bowl, combine Low-Carb Bake Mix, page 64, baking soda and salt. Stir into wet ingredients (dough will be fairly stiff). Stir in chocolate chips and nuts.

Drop by rounded tablespoonfuls (20 mL) onto ungreased cookie sheets.

Bake 8 to 10 minutes in 375°F (190°C) oven or until light brown. Cool slightly. Place cookies on wire rack to cool completely.

Helpful Hints: *I made these with $^1/_2$ tsp (2 mL) salt and they were wonderful in my opinion, however you could reduce the salt by half, if you like. SPLENDA® Granular does not cut the saltiness in the way that sugar does, and most times one has to reduce the salt in old favorite recipes, where sugar is replaced with the sweetener.

**Chocolate chips sweetened with sucralose are now available by Carbsense.com – called Minicarb® chocolate chips (see a complete listing of online retailers: (www.carbsense.com/online_retailers.htm) I used net carbs in the recipe.

GINGER HEARTS

Lovely treat for your low-carbing girlfriend who has just had a baby. Choose to make the frosting pink or blue. Layer between wax paper in a pretty tin, once frosting has set a little harder. Children love these cookies.

2$^1/_3$ cups Low-Carb Bake Mix, (575 mL)
  Page 64
1$^1/_4$ cups SPLENDA$^®$ Granular (300 mL)
2 tbsp vital wheat gluten (25 mL)
1 tbsp ground ginger (15 mL)
1 tsp baking powder (5 mL)
1 tsp cinnamon (5 mL)
$^1/_4$ tsp salt (1 mL)
$^1/_4$ cup regular cream cheese (50 mL)
$^1/_2$ cup butter* cut up, placed (125 mL)
  in plastic wrap in freezer 30 minutes
3 tbsp ice cold water (45 mL)

Frosting:
1 cup Confectioner's Sugar (250 mL)
  Substitute, page 97
2 tbsp whipping cream (25 mL)
2 tbsp butter (25 mL)
$^1/_2$ tsp vanilla extract (2 mL)
A few drops red or blue food coloring

Yield: 56 cookies
1 cookie
54.6 calories
2.6 g protein
4.1 g fat
1.9 g carbs

In food processor with S-blade, combine Low-Carb Bake Mix, page 64, SPLENDA$^®$ Granular, vital wheat gluten, ginger, baking powder, cinnamon and salt. Add cream cheese; process. Add frozen butter; process. Add ice cold water; process. Sprinkle counter with vanilla whey protein or roll dough out between two pieces of wax paper to about $^1/_8$-inch (0.5 cm) thickness. Using a heart-shaped cookie cutter {about 2-inches (5 cm) in size} cut out little hearts. Lift with a flat, very thin spatula and transfer to ungreased cookie sheets.

Bake in 400°F (200°C) oven 6 minutes, or until brown underneath.

Frosting: In clean food processor bowl, using S-blade, process Confectioner's Sugar Substitute, page 97, whipping cream, butter and vanilla extract. Add food coloring one drop at a time while processing, until the desired color is achieved. Pipe a tiny rosette on each cookie. If desired, pipe 2 rosettes on the hearts (extra frosting will be required).

Helpful Hint: It's important to measure the amount of butter on the demarcated line on the foil covering the block of butter or weigh 4 oz (113 g) of butter.

PECAN CRESCENT COOKIES

These shortbread cookies are bound to be a hit.

1 cup butter (250 mL)
  (no substitutes), softened
$^3/_4$ cup SPLENDA® Granular (175 mL)
$1^1/_2$ tsp vanilla extract (7 mL)
$2^1/_4$ cups Low-Carb Bake Mix, (550 mL)
  page 64
1 cup finely chopped pecans (250 mL)
2 tbsp Confectioner's Sugar (25 mL)
  Substitute, page 97

Yield: 60 plus cookies
1 cookie
61.0 calories
1.9 g protein
5.6 g fat
1.1 g carbs

In food processor with S-blade or in bowl with electric mixer, cream butter, SPLENDA® Granular and vanilla extract. Add half Low-Carb Bake Mix, page 64; process. Repeat. Stir in pecans.

Using heaped teaspoonfuls of dough, form $2^1/_2$ –inch (6 cm) logs and shape into crescents (like the shape of a crescent moon with a convex and concave edge). Place on ungreased cookie sheets and bake in 325°F (160°C) oven 12 minutes, or until set and light brown underneath. Let cool on cookie sheets 2 minutes. Transfer to wire racks. When completely cool, dust with Confectioner's Sugar Substitute, page 97.

~~Bits & Bites~~

Being metabolically resistant to weight loss has its advantages. The fat fast (outlined in More Splendid Low-Carbing, with menus and recipes, etc.) is only for these people (it can be dangerous for those who are not metabolically resistant to weight loss) and used just before one's period, it prevents the usual water weight gain and makes one feel wonderful. You may even lose weight!

SNOWY CINNAMON BALLS

Very more-ish! The centers should be soft with a strong cinnamon flavor. Do not overbake. Mine were done in 12 minutes. Best fresh. Freeze leftover cookies.

1¹/₂ cups ground almonds (375 mL)
16 SPLENDA® packets (125 mL)
1 tbsp ground cinnamon (15 mL)
2 egg whites (use large eggs)
2 tbsp Confectioner's Sugar (25 mL)
 Substitute, page 97

Yield: 18 cookies
1 cookie
54.8 calories
2.3 g protein
4.1 g fat
2.1 g carbs

In medium bowl, combine ground almonds, SPLENDA® and cinnamon. In food processor, with whipping assembly, whip egg whites until stiff. Fold egg whites into almond mixture to form stiff dough. Using 2 teaspoonfuls of dough, form small, smooth balls. Place on lightly greased cookie sheet. Bake in 350°F (180°C) oven 12 to 15 minutes, or until light brown underneath.

Roll balls in Confectioner's Sugar, page 97.

PEANUT BUTTER CHEWIES

Rich, satisfying peanut butter squares.

1 cup butter (250 mL)
 (2 sticks)
1 cup peanut, OR almond butter (250 mL)
3 cups SPLENDA® Granular (750 mL)
2¹/₄ cups Low-Carb Bake Mix, (550 mL)
 page 64
3 large eggs, fork beaten
1 tbsp molasses, optional (15 mL)
2 tsp vanilla extract (10 mL)

Yield: 54 squares
1 square/without molasses
89.1/88.2 calories
3.2/3.2 g protein
7.3/7.3 g fat
2.7/2.5 g carbs

In nonstick saucepan, melt butter and peanut butter (peanut butter does not have to melt completely). Remove from heat. Add SPLENDA® Granular, Low-Carb Bake Mix, page 64, eggs, molasses (if using) and vanilla extract. Stir to combine all at once.

Pour into greased 9 x 13 inch (23 x 33 cm) glass baking dish. Bake in 350°F (180°C) oven 25 to 30 minutes, or until edges are turning brown. Let cool to room temperature. Refrigerate until thoroughly chilled. Cut into squares.

COCONUTTY LEMON SQUARES

Lemon and coconut are a lovely combination. Watch these disappear.

Graham Cracker-Like Crust:
1 cup Low-Carb Bake Mix, (250 mL)
  page 64
1 cup ground almonds (250 mL)
$^1/_2$ cup butter, melted (125 mL)
2 SPLENDA® packets

Filling:
8 eggs, lightly beaten
$1^3/_4$ cups SPLENDA® Granular (425 mL)
$^3/_4$ cup lemon juice, (175 mL)
  (freshly squeezed, if possible)
1 tbsp grated lemon peel (15 mL)
$^1/_3$ cup Low-Carb Bake Mix, page 64 (75 mL)
$^1/_2$ tsp baking powder (2 mL)

Coconut Topping:
$^2/_3$ cup finely desiccated, unsweetened coconut (150 mL)
$^1/_3$ cup SPLENDA® Granular (75 mL)

Yield: 40 squares
1 square
83.1 calories
3.3 g protein
6.6 g fat
2.5 g carbs

Graham Cracker-like Crust: In medium bowl, combine Low-Carb Bake Mix, page 64, ground almonds, butter and SPLENDA®. Press in bottom of 9 x 13-inch (23 x 33 cm) glass baking dish. Bake in 350°F (180°C) oven 12 minutes, or until light, golden brown.

Filling: In large bowl, combine eggs, SPLENDA® Granular, lemon juice and lemon peel. Gradually whisk in Low-Carb Bake Mix, page 64 and baking powder. Pour carefully over cooled crust. Bake in 325°F (160°C) oven 10 minutes, add Coconut Topping and bake another 10 minutes, or until coconut starts turning light brown in places. Let cool and refrigerate.

Coconut Topping: In small bowl, combine coconut and SPLENDA® Granular.

~~Bits & Bites~~
Baking with SPLENDA® Granular in chocolate recipes requires some skill and practice to prevent an overly bitter product.

CHOCOLATE MACAROON SQUARES

A substantial coconut macaroon base with a delicious, thick chocolate coating. This would make an attractive square on a plate with several similar goodies.

Macaroon Crust:
2 cups fine coconut (500 mL)
  (unsweetened)
$^1/_2$ cup vanilla whey protein (125 mL)
24 SPLENDA® packets
4 oz butter, melted (113 g)
2 extra-large eggs, fork beaten

Topping:
$^2/_3$ cup whipping cream (150 mL)
$^2/_3$ cup butter, melted (150 mL)
$^1/_4$ cup Da Vinci® Sugar Free Vanilla Syrup (50 mL)
2 cups SPLENDA® Granular (500 mL)
$^2/_3$ cup vanilla whey protein (150 mL)
$^2/_3$ cup skim, OR whole milk powder (150 mL)
$^1/_4$ tsp Thickening Agent, page 62 (1 mL)
2 oz unsweetened chocolate (60 g)
0.5 oz cocoa butter (15 g)

> **Yield:** 54 squares
> 1 square
> 95.5 calories
> 2.4 g protein
> 8.4 g fat
> **2.4 g carbs**

Macaroon Crust: In medium bowl, combine coconut, vanilla whey protein and SPLENDA®. Add butter and eggs; stir well. Pour into 9 x 13-inch (23 x 33 cm) glass baking dish and using plastic wrap, press crust out evenly. Bake in 350°F (180°C) oven 10 minutes.

Topping: In blender, combine whipping cream, butter, Da Vinci® Sugar Free Vanilla Syrup, SPLENDA® Granular, vanilla whey protein, skim or whole milk powder and Thickening Agent, page 62. Blend until smooth. In cereal bowl, melt chocolate 2 minutes on high power in microwave oven. In separate cereal bowl, melt cocoa butter $2^1/_2$ minutes or more on high power in microwave oven. Add melted chocolate and melted cocoa butter to blender; blend until smooth. Spread chocolate over cooled macaroon crust. Chill. Cut into squares.

Variation: Da Vinci® Alternative: Use water, $^1/_4$ tsp (1 mL) vanilla extract and 1 SPLENDA® packet (optional).

Helpful Hint: Cereal bowls and contents will be very hot after microwaving. Be careful and use oven mitts.

~~Bits & Bites~~
Low-carb ice creams are an easy and satisfying treat.

105

CHUNKY CHOCOLATE PECAN SQUARES

A decadent treat that makes a good addition to a party plate of squares.

Graham Cracker-like Crust:

²/₃ cup Low-Carb Bake Mix, (150 mL)
  Page 64
²/₃ cup ground almonds (150 mL)
¹/₃ cup butter, melted (75 mL)
2 SPLENDA® packets

Filling:

3 eggs
¹/₂ cup Ketogenics® Sugar Free Pancake Syrup, OR (125 mL)
  Maple Syrup, page 172, *Splendid Low-Carbing*
¹/₃ cup SPLENDA® Granular (75 mL)
2 tbsp butter, melted (25 mL)
¹/₂ tsp vanilla extract (2 mL)
1 cup sugar free chocolate chips (250 mL)
  (sweetened)
³/₄ cup chopped pecans (175 mL)

Yield: 25 squares
1 square
100.4 calories
3.0 g protein
7.7 g fat
1.6 g carbs

Graham Cracker-like Crust: In medium bowl, combine Low-Carb Bake Mix, page 64, ground almonds, butter and SPLENDA®. Press into an 8-inch (20 cm) square glass dish. Bake in 350°F (180°C) oven 10 minutes.

Filling: In medium bowl, beat eggs with fork. Stir in Ketogenics® Sugar Free Pancake Syrup, SPLENDA® Granular, butter and vanilla extract. Stir in chocolate chips and pecans. Pour over prepared crust.

Bake in 350°F (180°C) oven 25 minutes, or until filling has set. Cool in pan on wire rack. Cut into squares and refrigerate.

Helpful Hints: These squares can be frozen. 1 cup (250 mL) Chocolate chips = 6 oz (180 g).

~~Bits & Bites~~

Cookies are usually stored at room temperature in an airtight container. They usually freeze well in airtight containers or freezer bags up to 4 months.

AWARD-WINNING BROWNIES

Excellent, dense and fudgey brownies!

4 eggs
1 cup unsalted butter, melted (250 mL)
$^1/_4$ cup Da Vinci® Sugar Free (50 mL)
  Vanilla Syrup, OR water, $^1/_4$ tsp (1 mL)
  vanilla extract & 1 SPLENDA® packet
$^1/_4$ tsp chocolate extract (1 mL)
$1^3/_4$ cups Low-Carb Bake Mix, (425 mL)
  page 64
$^1/_3$ cup Dutch cocoa (75 mL)
1 cup SPLENDA® Granular (250 mL)
24 SPLENDA® packets
1 tsp baking powder (5 mL)
$^3/_8$ tsp salt (1.5 mL)
Condensed Milk Chocolate Frosting, page 96

Yield: 40 (8 x 5) brownies
1 brownie
119.2 calories
3.7 g protein
10.5 g fat
2.9 g carbs

In food processor or in bowl with electric mixer, process eggs. Add butter, Da Vinci® Sugar Free Vanilla Syrup (or water, vanilla extract and SPLENDA®) and chocolate extract. Process on slow speed. In medium bowl, combine Low-Carb Bake Mix, page 64, cocoa, SPLENDA® Granular, SPLENDA®, baking powder and salt. Add to food processor and process until smooth. Spread in greased 9 x 13-inch (2 L) glass baking dish. Bake in 350°F (180°C) oven 17 to 20 minutes, or until dinner knife inserted into brownies comes out clean.

Condensed Milk Chocolate Frosting: Prepare as directed on page 96. Spread frosting over warm brownies in baking dish. Refrigerate and cut into squares when chilled.

Helpful Hints: For a sweeter result in any of my brownies or chocolate recipes, try combining sweeteners. I've heard good things about Erythritol (a sugar alcohol), which does not cause digestive problems, however, it produces a "cooling effect" in the mouth, therefore, use a small amount in combination with SPLENDA® Granular to minimize that cooling effect. I find my chocolate recipes sweet enough and the packets I use sometimes certainly pack a slightly sweeter punch, however, some people really miss the sweeter taste of sugar in chocolate recipes and for those people my suggestion is to combine sweeteners.

My husband liked these more after they were refrigerated for a day. These brownies freeze well in an airtight plastic container. Place in one layer. Microwave one brownie 25 to 30 seconds or allow time for thawing naturally.

INDEX